ST. MARTIN'S

TRUE CRIME
CLASSICS

TITLES BY KEN ENGLADE

FROM THE TRUE CRIME LIBRARY OF
ST. MARTIN'S PAPERBACKS

CELLAR
OF
HORROR

KEN ENGLADE

St. Martin's Paperbacks

CELLAR OF HORROR

Copyright © 1988 by Ken Englade.

Cover photo of Gary Heidnik courtesy AP/Wide World Photos.
Cover photo of stairs © Michael Gesinger/Graphistock.

ISBN: 0-312-92929-3
EAN: 80312-92929-9

Printed in the United States of America

St. Martin's Paperbacks edition / March 1989

St. Martin's Paperbacks are published by St. Martin's Press, 175 Fifth Avenue, New York, NY 10010.

15 14 13 12 11

For my patient and loving wife, Sara, whose support was invaluable.

Acknowledgments

This book could not have been written without the aid of Chuck Peruto and his partner, Jack Fognano, who went beyond the legal issues and helped me see the human side of a very complicated story. Likewise, for helping me feel my way around an unfamiliar city, I owe a special thanks to Mildred Keil and Hilda Schoenwetter.

For sharing the efforts of his reporting I am especially grateful to Kurt Heine of the *Philadelphia Daily News.* For helping fill in the blank spots, my thanks to Juan Guerra of Channel 29; Doris Zibulka and her father, Warren Hensman; the men of the Sheriff's Department, especially Deputy Jim Lee; and Judge Lynne Abraham's staff and others around City Hall.

For helping educate me about the intricacies of Gary Heidnik's complex personality, I owe special thanks to Jack Apsche.

I am particularly grateful as well to Todd Moritz for his technical support, and to Diana Clark, Mike Webb and Katherine Krell for sharing their expertise in the insanity defense. Advice and counsel came from many sources, but I am especially indebted to my editor, Charlie Spicer, and Betsy Graham, David Snell and Rick Gove.

Prologue

February 10, 1987
5:05 P.M.

Officer Julio Aponte shook his head. "No," the rookie cop said emphatically. "I can't do it. Not without checking with my supervisor."

It was cold. Too cold to stand shivering on the porch of a beat-up house in a gone-to-seed neighborhood in North Philadelphia arguing with a civilian. But Warren Hensman was insistent. A cop himself once in California, where it never got this cold, Hensman wanted only one thing from Aponte. He wanted him to break into this house to see if the man who lived there, a weird duck named Gary Heidnik, was alive and well.

Hensman and a few other neighbors were worried. They hadn't seen Heidnik for several days, and there was this bad smell, this *really* bad smell, emanating from his house. Hensman knew Heidnik was depressed. When his neighbor's Filipino wife had left him a year before, he had choked down a six-week supply of Thorazine—almost forty times the lethal dose—and nearly died. Betty had come back after that, but now she was gone again, this time apparently for good. There was no telling what Heidnik was likely to do. When this stench seeped out of the house and settled over the neighborhood like a malodorous fog, they called the cops.

Aponte's shift started an hour before, and already it looked like his day was off to a crummy start. He had been peacefully patrolling his assigned sector in the notorious Twenty-sixth District, Philadelphia's dope capital, when his radio crackled.

"Check on the well-being of a person and a foul odor at 3520 North Marshall Street," the dispatcher ordered.

Now that he was here, what could he do? He didn't have to put a stethoscope to the door to hear the hard rock blasting away. Despite the music, when he listened carefully he thought he could detect the sounds of someone moving around inside. But no one answered when he knocked. He went to a window and tried peeping in, but the shades were drawn skin tight. Even the rips were covered with duct tape. He walked around the left side of the house, where a driveway separated 3520 from Hensman's residence, and banged on the back door. Again, he got no response. The shade was not down all the way on one of the back windows, and when he looked in he could see into the kitchen. It looked normal enough. On the top of the stove was a large aluminum stockpot, which was frothing over.

Except for the smell being particularly pungent at the back, Aponte didn't notice anything unusual. The smell was worse than anything he had ever before encountered, but in this neighborhood nothing surprised him. On that February evening it was just another annoyance that he could well do without, just as he could do without Hensman hassling him to knock down the door just because his neighbor wanted to be left alone.

It wasn't just Hensman either. Standing there waiting for him to do something was Hensman's daughter, Doris Zibulka, whose house abutted Heidnik's, and a few others from up and down the street. They demanded that Officer Aponte kick down the door.

"That smell is so bad it's making my eyes water," complained Zibulka, a normally jovial mother of three young girls. "I can't cook in my house because the smell makes me nauseated."

"Yeah," chorused the others. "Do something. It smells like burning bodies."

Aponte looked at the door. It was metal. Could he break it down? Fat chance, he thought. He looked at the windows. They were protected by sturdy iron burglar bars. No hope there either.

"Look," he said, trying to be reasonable, "I'll call in and try to get a supervisor out here."

Turning, he walked the thirty yards to his car and was explaining his problem to the dispatcher when the door creaked open and a white man with a beard and piercing pale eyes poked his head out. Everybody jumped.

"Good God!" Hensman cried in relief, smiling at Gary Heidnik. "You're all right."

"Sure, I'm all right," Heidnik replied affably, "Everything's okay."

"Cancel that request," Aponte said into the microphone.

"We thought you were dead," said Hensman. "There's that terrible smell and we thought it was you."

"Oh no, I'm okay," Heidnik repeated. "I just burned my dinner is all."

Aponte studied Heidnik. He certainly wasn't dead; in fact, he looked pretty healthy. He wasn't ranting or raving, and he didn't talk crazy. As far as the smell went, he had explained that satisfactorily. He himself had seen the boiling pot. You can't arrest a guy for being a lousy cook.

Aponte sighed. That turned out to be an easy assignment. Jumping into his blue and white, he drove off.

If Aponte had gone inside that house that day, he would have gotten the shock of his young life. In the basement he would have found four semi-nude young black women, tethered like livestock with heavy chains. In the oven he would have found a human rib cage burning to a cinder. And if he had looked in the bubbling caldron to see what Heidnik was having for "dinner," his blond hair might have turned gray. Boiling away on the back burner of Gary Heidnik's stove was the head of a young black woman.

"She came in, and as we were walking up the steps, she was rambling on, you know, talking real fast about this guy having three girls chained up in the basement of this house and she was held hostage for four months . . . She said that he was beating them, raping them, had them eating dead people, just like he was a cold-blooded nut. Dogs was in the yard eating people bones. I just thought she was crazy. I really didn't believe it, and I still don't believe this shit."

Vincent Nelson, Josefina Rivera's boyfriend

Chapter 1

November 26, 1986

Josefina Rivera was having a rough night. In another hour it would be Thanksgiving, but so far she didn't have a lot to be thankful for.

She was still fuming about her argument with her boyfriend, a thirty-year-old black man named Vincent Nelson. She stomped out of his apartment in a huff. Then, when she went back an hour later to apologize, they started fighting all over again. That's when she said to hell with it and left a second time, figuring she might as well go to work.

Pacing back and forth at the corner of Third and Girard, she cursed under her breath and kicked at the trash littering the sidewalk: empty coffee cups; bright aluminum cans, which would soon be scooped up like treasure by neighborhood bums on their nightly rounds; and soggy mounds of what had been sheets from that afternoon's *Daily News,* now reduced to mush by a heavy, early-evening shower.

The rain had been the forerunner of a Canadian cold front barreling down the Eastern seaboard, bringing a jolting taste of winter to Philadelphia's northside slums. As she performed a little hop-and-skip around the puddles of dirty water, she burrowed deeper into her thin windbreaker, seeking relief from the plunging temperatures.

All the while, even as she swore against Nelson and the weather, she kept an eye on the street, sensitive to the cars that braked and cruised slowly past while the drivers gave her the once-over. Every time one of them seemed about to stop, she made an effort to look cheerful, flashing a fake, airline-hostess smile.

What the drivers saw was a thin, striking-looking woman of medium height clad in sneakers and skin-tight jeans. Josefina Rivera had fine, well-developed features, inherited from her Puerto Rican father rather than her black mother. Her nose was long and straight, her lips pencil thin, and her skin the color of coffee with double cream. Fortunately for her, the dim light hid the hard lines at the corners of her mouth and the flat glint in her eyes; the cool stare that was much older than her twenty-five years. When it looked as though a potential john was really interested, Rivera gave her head a quick jerk, setting the waves in her outsized wig jiggling like a fat man's stomach.

Usually she had no trouble attracting men, but tonight was exceptionally slow. As the evening wore on, she became increasingly desperate. It was cold and wet on the glum street corner, but she couldn't afford to give up yet. She didn't want to quit without at least one quick trick. She needed the money. A rabbit-fast liaison in a seedy motel or the back of a car would make her night, give her enough money for a hot Turkey Day dinner.

As she reached the edge of her self-defined boundary and reversed her course to make another circuit, a pair of headlights glared, went slightly past her and stopped. Glancing over, she opened her eyes slightly in surprise when she saw that it was a shiny new pewter-over-white Cadillac Coupe De Ville, complete with gleaming continental kit.

As she stared, the window glided down and a man

spoke. It was a white man's voice, soft and low. "Hi," he said, leaning forward. "You hustling?"

"Yeah," Rivera responded, straining to see inside. Despite the gloom, she caught a reflection of light off a big, expensive-looking watch on the man's left wrist.

"How much you want?" he asked affably.

She named a figure and he made a counter offer: "Will you take twenty?"

It didn't take her long to decide. In response, she opened the door and slid into the passenger seat, noticing as she did the initials GMH painted on the door in flowing blue script. The smell inside the car was intoxicating, an overwhelming aroma of leather and wax. The Caddy was only nine days off the dealer's floor.

"My name's Gary," the man said.

"I'm Nicole," she answered, using her favorite alias. Nicole was a nice name, she felt, infinitely fancier than Josefina. To her it had class; it went better with her image of herself as a slightly exotic hooker.

"I want to make a quick stop first," the man said as he pulled away. A few minutes later he aimed the big car into the crowded lot of a McDonald's.

When he walked inside, she went with him. He bought coffee but offered her nothing. Clutching his steaming cup tightly in his right fist, he strolled to a back table and sat facing the parking lot. She slid into a chair across from him.

In the restaurant's bright light she could see him clearly, appraising with interest the thick gold chain and gold cross visible through the open neck of his plaid flannel shirt. In counterpoint to the jewelry and the heavy watch, which she now saw carried the Rolex name, the man wore an inexpensive cowhide jacket with leather fringes down the arms, the same kind of garment Jon Voight favored in the movie *Midnight Cowboy*.

The jacket was stained, and in spots the suede had rubbed through, leaving irregular shiny patches that looked like moth holes. It smelled, too, of sweat and grease, a fact evident now that it wasn't camouflaged by the new-car scent.

The man, Rivera noticed, was not the cleanest john she had ever done business with. His dark beard was neatly trimmed and his hair had recently been styled, but now it was unwashed, hanging in greasy ringlets over his ears. His shirt had a slept-in look, and his jeans, although fairly new, were marked with traces of oil and dirt. He had a strong jaw, though, and a straight nose. His most arresting feature was his eyes; they were as expressionless as two blue glass marbles. Looking into them, a shiver ran up her spine.

"What's your name?" she asked.

"I already told you," he said. "Gary."

"Gary what?" she persisted.

"Gary Heidnik," he said, lapsing into silence, quietly sipping from his steaming cup.

"Let's go," he said after a few minutes.

"Where are we going?"

"My house," he answered, already heading for the door.

Heidnik pulled out of the lot and pointed the car north, deeper into the slum district. Speeding recklessly down the potholed streets, one foot on the brake and one on the gas, Heidnik said nothing as they maneuvered through an expanse of row houses, block after block of dwellings sitting literally on the cracked sidewalks.

In years past, this section of Philadelphia had been home to hardworking blue-collar immigrants, Germans for the most part, who took pride in their surroundings and kept the streets as spotless as their houses. When these immigrants and their descendants abandoned the neighborhood for the suburbs, the blacks and Hispanics who moved in were not as fastidious.

By 1986 the neighborhood had earned the nickname

"The OK Corral" because of a highly publicized, middle-of-the-street shootout between would-be drug lords—an incident that left several bystanders wounded while the participants escaped unscathed. In a demonstration of perverse pride, neighborhood toughs sewed the name "OK Corral" on their jackets and strutted the title proudly through the neighborhood, especially when they worked the corners hawking crack, coke, and pot to passing motorists.

When they got to North Marshall Street, Heidnik took a sharp left, nearly clipping an abandoned Chevy parked at the curb. The car's windows were broken out and its wheels had been removed. All vital parts had long ago been carted off. At one point someone had attempted to torch the vehicle, and the path of the flames were still visible on the rusting exterior.

Just past the wreck, Heidnik turned left again, swinging through a gap in a waist-high chain-link fence into a trash-littered yard. The number on the post in front was 3520. Gary Heidnik was home.

Chapter 2

Number 3520 was an anomaly. For blocks around, in all directions, there were nothing but row houses; street after street of grim, deteriorating dwellings lying on their deathbeds with their chins in the street. But Heidnik's house was different. It was not only set back a dozen yards from the sidewalk, but it was unattached on one side, leaving enough space for a small yard and a driveway, which led to the rarest structure of all, considering the neighborhood: a garage.

In Heidnik's case the garage was a ramshackle building with a definite starboard list; a fragile-looking structure of badly weathered board topped with a row of barbed wire to keep trespassers from climbing over from the alley. He also had lined the inside of the creaky doors with metal after a group of neighborhood punks fired several shots at the building the previous summer. One of the bullets had damaged a Cadillac Heidnik had parked inside, the predecessor of his current De Ville. He had vowed that would never happen again. Heidnik was very attached to his cars.

As Heidnik eased into the garage, Rivera noticed a dark shape occupying the other half of the building. Barely visible in the dark, it was a 1971 Rolls-Royce—Heidnik's pride and joy. He had paid $17,000 in cash for the vehicle less than a year before, but in the few short months he owned it he had managed to burn out the engine and transmission, which he replaced with Chevrolet parts. Unsatisfied, too, with the finely crafted radio that came with the vehicle, Heidnik had mounted a cheap tape player under the dash. Scattered around on the Rolls' floor were inexpensive cassettes of music he had taped himself.

As he hurried toward the house, anxious to get out of the rising wind, Heidnik pulled a ring from his pocket and twirled it until he came to a stumpy piece of metal with an unevenly serrated edge. Rivera eyed it curiously.

"What's that?" she asked.

"A key," he grunted.

"I never seen a key like that before."

"I made it," Heidnik said. "I put the regular key halfway in and sawed it off. The front half stays in the lock permanently."

"Why'd you do that?" she inquired.

"So no other key except mine will work," he replied, swinging open the door and stepping in front of her into a small kitchen, the walls of which were half covered with pennies which had been meticulously glued into place.

"This way," he said, leading her into a sparsely furnished living room.

On one wall, under a heavily barred window, was a battered orange couch, stained and swaybacked. Opposite the couch was a stand holding a stereo tape deck and turntable, a TV and a VCR. Next to the stand was a cabinet jammed with dozens of videotape cassettes, each with a handwritten label.

"You want to see a movie?" he asked.

Rivera glanced at the titles; she could see he was heavily into porno flicks, horror films, and sappy comedies. Disinterested, she made a show of looking at her watch.

"Let's skip the movie," she said. "I'm running a little short on time."

Catching the quick flash of anger that jumped across Heidnik's face, she hastily added: "I have three children at home, and my babysitter leaves at midnight."

It was a lie, but Heidnik didn't know that. She was beginning to feel very uncomfortable, and all she wanted to do was finish the job, collect her money, and go back to see if she could straighten out her disagreement with Vincent Nelson.

"Okay." Heidnik shrugged, apparently unoffended. Turning on his heel, he led the way up a flight of rickety stairs. As they entered a narrow hallway at the head of the steps, Rivera did a double take. The wall there, instead of being covered with pennies, had been partially papered with one- and five-dollar bills.

"In here," Heidnik said, opening a door into a room containing a waterbed, a dresser, and two chairs. "Here's your money," he said, digging in his pocket and extracting a soiled twenty dollar bill, which he handed to Rivera. Without another word, he peeled off his clothes and jumped into bed.

Rivera put the bill on top of the dresser, slipped out of her shirt and jeans, and climbed in with Heidnik.

After a few minutes of active but emotionless coupling, Heidnik stood and walked across the room toward his pile of clothes. Rivera got up, too, and reached for her shirt. She had it on and was about to step into her jeans when she felt a pair of strong hands clamp securely around her throat. Twisting, she looked up into Heidnik's eyes, which seemed colder than ever. Without expression, he tightened his grip, slowly squeezing her life away. Just before she passed out, she squeaked her surrender.

"All right," she croaked. "I'll do anything you say, but don't hurt me."

When Heidnik relaxed his pressure, she sagged to the

floor. As she fell, she realized he had slipped a handcuff onto her right wrist.

"Stand up and put your hands behind your back," Heidnik ordered.

When she complied, he slipped the twin cuff on her other wrist. Dragging her over to the dresser, he scooped up the bill he had given her earlier and returned it to his pocket. Then he pushed her out the door, down the stairs, and through the living room and kitchen. He opened another door and she saw a second flight of stairs, these narrower than the first and unprotected by a banister. Pushing her again, he forced her down into a cold, damp, dimly-lit room that smelled strongly of mildew and dust. The chill air reminded Rivera that she was wearing nothing but a shirt. As her feet hit the icy concrete floor, she jumped in surprise. Then she started shivering.

"Over there," Heidnik said, maneuvering her toward a lumpy, bare mattress pushed into one corner of the small room.

"I can't see out of my right eye," she complained.

"Shut up," he told her.

"My vision is blurred," she insisted.

He grabbed a piece of lumber that was lying among other bits of debris on the dirty floor. "If you don't shut up, I'm going to hit you," he said, waving the club.

She shut up.

Walking across the room, Heidnik picked up a small cardboard box and extracted from it a metal rod that had been bent in the middle to form a skinny U. Looking closely, Rivera saw that each end of the rod was threaded. Actually, the device was a commercially-made product called a muffler clamp. Mechanics attach them to the underside of cars to cradle and support a vehicle's exhaust pipe.

Heidnik ran one end of the clamp through a heavy chain, which he pulled from another box, and then forced

the clamp over Rivera's ankle. A small metal bar fit between the two prongs to seal off the open end of the *U*.
He dug in the box again and came up with two nuts,
which he screwed onto the threads after first wetting
them down with super glue. From out of nowhere, it
seemed, he pulled a hair dryer and aimed that at the glue
to make it dry faster. Then he repeated the procedure
with a second clamp.

While Rivera stood frozen in shock, Heidnik flipped
the loose end of the chain over a five-inch-thick pipe that
came out of the ceiling and ran across the room into the
opposite wall.

Standing back to survey his handiwork, Heidnik nodded in satisfaction. "Sit down," he told her, pointing at
the mattress.

When she did, he stretched out beside her, put his head
in her naked lap and went to sleep.

Chapter 3

Gary Heidnik had a thing for November. Important things happened to him then. He was born in that month, in 1943. He faced his first criminal charges in November 1978. He took Josefina Rivera captive in November eight years later. He would take one more captive before the month rolled over. And in November 1961 he had committed what may well have been his last-ever conventional act. One week after his eighteenth birthday he joined the Army.

Each of these events was significant. Each was traumatic. Each was a starting point or a turning point. Come December, in 1961, 1978, and 1986, Gary Heidnik may as well have been born again, because his life was changed forever.

Thousands of teenagers join the Army every year. For most of them it is a bittersweet occasion. They're growing up. They're leaving family and friends, at least temporarily. But there was nothing temporary about it for Gary Heidnik. When he rolled out of Cleveland, Ohio, bound for Fort Leonard Wood, Missouri, he wasn't ever going back. Well, maybe once. But only for a few days. Later, he would tell psychiatrists his father would fight with him. Disown him. His father admitted they didn't speak for twenty-five years. They still don't. His father told reporters he has no use for his son. And Gary has none for him. When Gary Heidnik ended up in jail, charged with all sorts of monstrous crimes, his father had no sympathy. If he did those things, the father said, he hoped they gave him the electric chair. He would even pull the switch.

Father and son had been fighting all their lives. Gary Michael Heidnik was Michael Heidnik's firstborn. Gary's father was a tool-and-die maker in the Cleveland suburb of Eastlake. His mother Ellen, a not unattractive woman of Creole descent, was a beautician. They lived in a middle-class house in a middle-class subdivision. They probably were not very happy. Not really. Not ever.

A year and a half after Gary was born, Ellen gave birth to another boy. They named him Terry. As they grew, Gary and Terry fought. And they both fought their father. Except Gary and Terry maintained their relationship longer. The Terry–Michael equation was just as unbalanced as the Gary–Michael one. Terry later claimed that his father had broken all relations with him, too, just as he had with Gary.

According to the records, Gary and Terry didn't match with Ellen either. Neither did Michael. In 1946, when Gary was two and Terry was a toddler, Michael and Ellen split. In her divorce petition, Ellen accused Michael of "gross neglect of duty." Michael said she was a "wild woman." And "a boozer" to boot.

Gary and Terry went with their mother, who had remarried. It started a pattern. Before she committed suicide in 1970, she would marry three more times. Her last two husbands would be black.

Gary and Terry lived with Ellen until it was about time for Gary to start school. Then they went to live with Michael, who also had remarried. Gary and Terry didn't get along with their stepmother worth a flip. But their relationship with Michael was even worse. They both said their father was a ferocious disciplinarian. When he wet his bed, Gary claimed in later conversations with psychologists, his father made him hang the soiled sheet out the window of his second story bedroom for all the world to see. Gary also claimed that when Michael thought his son was *really* bad, he'd hang him out the window too. Grab him by his ankles and dangle him headfirst twenty feet or more off the ground. One time, according to Terry, when he was mad at both Gary and Terry, Michael painted bull's-eyes on the seats of their jeans and sent them off to school. In his more gracious moments, Gary would describe his father as an "Archie Bunker type" or a "cold fish." The psychologist to whom he told this thought those were extraordinarily benign descriptions. Michael Heidnik, 74, contended his children were raised in a normal household, as he has said since his son was arrested on March 25, 1987. He denied he had beaten them or taught them to be prejudiced. Heidnik described the environment in which his sons were raised as "average."

"He was an average kid," he said of Gary. "He went to school. He played baseball like the other kids, but, Jesus, he must have lost his buttons."

Gary had other troubles besides those with his father. According to Terry, Gary was ridiculed because he had an oddly shaped head. The other kids called him "football head." Terry said it was the result of an accident. When Gary was in an early grade he fell out of a tree, flat on his crown. After that, Terry said, Gary's personality changed. That has the ring of an apocryphal story. As an adult, Terry would also have mental problems. He later told police he had spent considerable time in mental institutions and had tried suicide several times. The interesting thing is, *he* never fell out of a tree.

Gary did what most boys who grew up in suburbia in the 40s and the 50s did. He joined the Boy Scouts and he worked at summer jobs. One summer he spent his vacation painting fire hydrants. He dated girls, but he was shy, so he didn't get around a lot.

He had two interests in life: business and the military. He devoured the financial sections of newspapers like other kids did comics. "One day," he used to say, "I'm going to be a millionaire." When he was in the eighth grade, he wore oversize military fatigues everywhere he went. His ambition, besides making a lot of money, was to go to West Point.

When he was in the ninth grade, Michael scraped up enough money to send him to military school. He picked the Staunton Military Academy in Virginia, a fairly prestigious school at the time. Its alumni include John Dean and Barry Goldwater. The school closed in 1976 but a former superintendent told the *Plain Dealer*, Gary's hometown newspaper, that during his two years there, Gary Heidnik scored "exceptionally fine marks" and was not a disciplinary problem.

It was roughly during that period, too, Gary later admitted to mental health professionals, that he made his first visit to a shrink. What prompted this has never been disclosed. Neither is it known how long the treatment lasted. Gary has revealed only one thing about that early encounter: He was never given any medication.

Maybe it was because he had simply burned out. Or perhaps the pressures were getting too great. Whatever, he dropped out of Staunton at the end of his junior year. He went back to the Cleveland suburbs, where he lived with Michael and a stepmother he thinks hated him. He enrolled in Eastlake's North High School but didn't remain long. Six weeks later he switched to East High School in Cleveland. That lasted a month. Then he joined the Army.

When he walked out the door of his suburban Ohio home on the cusp of winter in 1961, his psychological baggage was considerably heavier than the barracks bag he clutched in his hand. He was leaving his childhood behind, and he was damn glad of it.

Chapter 4

November 27, 1986

When Josefina Rivera awoke, she was alone in the cellar. She had no idea how long she had been asleep or how long her captor had been gone. Looking around, she saw an unmoving bulk in the far corner. Her heart leaped and she stifled a cry. Then, squinting, she saw that it was a washer-dryer. She sighed in relief.

There was a window in the room, located at head height a few feet from where she huddled in fear, but it had been boarded up so no light filtered in from outside. The only illumination came from a dim overhead bulb which threw long shadows around the depressing space. Across the room, farther than she could reach when she stretched her tether to its full length, was a white chest-style freezer. It looked like a coffin, she thought. Later—much later—it would prove to be just that. Virtually at her elbow was a battered pool table, its felt surface blotched and torn. She saw nothing to give her hope, nothing to cheer her up.

Hugging herself, she realized suddenly that she was still naked from the waist down and that she was cold. The floor and walls were bare concrete, which contributed to the damp chill that seeped into her bones.

One area caught her eye. At a spot not far away, the concrete on the floor had been broken up and there was a shallow pit in the dirt underneath. For a fleeting moment the word *grave* popped into her mind, but she dismissed it. The broken spot in the concrete was smaller than a washtub and not even that deep. She had no idea what it was for.

Letting her shoulders droop, she hugged her knees and tried to think about life in the outside world. She wondered if people living in real time were sitting down to a holiday feast. That thought reminded her that she was hungry; hungry enough, in fact, to eat an entire turkey, feathers and all.

As though in response to her thoughts, she heard the upstairs door open and Heidnik unexpectedly clump down the stairs. In his hand was her holiday meal: an egg sandwich and a glass of orange juice.

She looked at it suspiciously. She was hungry, but not that hungry. For all she knew, his offering was poisoned or drugged. He held it out to her. She shook her head. "I think I'll wait."

"Suit yourself," he said, turning and carrying it back upstairs. A few minutes later he returned, lugging a pick and shovel. The word *grave* flashed through her mind again.

Turning his back on her, Heidnik began digging at the earth in the spot where the concrete had been removed. First he deepened the hole, then he used the shovel as a scoop to widen the pit under the concrete that had not been chipped away.

As he worked, he talked. He told her what he wanted most in the world was to have a big family but that something always happened to ruin his plans. He told her that in his lifetime (he had celebrated his forty-third birthday six days earlier, but he didn't tell her that) he had fathered four children by four different women. But all four were now gone, taken away from him either by the mothers or by the authorities. He was particularly bitter about an experience with a woman named Anjeanette. They had a baby girl, but the state took her away immediately and put her in a foster home. Before he could have more children by her, he got into serious trouble for trying to help her sister escape from an institution. The sister, he said, was thirty-four years old and had willingly had sex with him, but they charged him with rape and sent him away to prison. When he returned four years later, Anje-anette had disappeared.

"Society owes me a wife and family," he told Rivera. "I want to get ten women and keep them here and get them all pregnant. Then, when they have babies, I want to raise those children here too. We'll be one big happy family."

Rivera shivered. He didn't have to tell her that she was Number One.

Heidnik put down the shovel and walked over to where she was sitting. Unzipping his pants, he pulled his penis out and ordered her to take it in her mouth. After a few minutes he inserted it in her vagina and pumped away until he climaxed. Then he went back upstairs.

Left on her own, Rivera started working on the nuts on her shackles. With some effort she freed her left ankle, giving her the mobility to scurry around the room as far as the chain would allow—about twelve feet. She went to the window and started working on the covering until she pried it open enough to see daylight. Desperately search-ing for a tool, she found a cue stick under the pool table and used that as a lever to force the covering back so she could open the window. Then, boosting herself up, she wiggled through the opening into the backyard. She crawled as far as the chain would stretch and started screaming.

Screams were not unusual in the OK Corral. All the time, day and night, someone was screaming. The resi-dents learned to ignore them; they became as much a part of the background noise as the squeal of tires and the boom of gunshots. Rivera yelled and yelled. She yelled until she was hoarse; until Heidnik heard her.

Red-faced, he raced into the yard and silenced her with a smack. Then he tried to shove her back through the hole she had climbed out of. She went limp and he couldn't get her back in. So he ran back inside, down the stairs. Grabbing the chain, he started hauling her in like a giant fish. Once he got her inside, he shoved her into the pit in the floor and dragged over a piece of plywood to put over the top. However, the hole wasn't deep enough to hold her. Even with her legs folded against her chest, her head stuck up too much for the board to lie flat. She started screaming again.

"I can't breathe," she pleaded. "I need air."

Heidnik shoved the board aside, grabbed her by her hair, and yanked her out of the pit. Then he picked up a stick and started beating her. When she whimpered surrender, he shoved her back in the pit, pulled the board over the opening and forced it down, making her bend her neck until her chin was on her chest. He put several bags of dirt on top to hold it in place, then left her alone again.

He came back a few minutes later with a radio, which he tuned to a rock station. Setting the volume all the way up, he left again and didn't come back for twenty-seven hours. She knew precisely how long it was because the station's deejays were fanatic about announcing the time.

A wave of frustration and depression swept over her. Never had she felt so frightened and dejected. Now, with the radio blasting away, even if she screamed, no one would ever hear her. For the first time she could remember, she cried with all her heart.

Chapter 5

January 1962

Gary Heidnik was a good soldier. He kept his nose clean. He stayed out of trouble. He saved his money. But he probably didn't make many friends.

After boot camp he asked to be sent to Military Police school. The Army turned him down. The minimum age for MPs was nineteen; Gary was barely eighteen. So he asked to be a stenographic clerk. The Army again said no. A parts clerk? No. A heavy-equipment operator? No. An electrician? Still no. What the Army said was: Gary, do we have a deal for you. We're going to make you a hospital corpsman. A medic. So Gary Heidnik shipped off to Fort Sam Houston in San Antonio, Texas, for training. When he graduated, his ticket was stamped "excellent" in both conduct and efficiency.

From what he said later, Gary Heidnik learned more than how to change bandages during medic training. Suddenly he had more money than ever before in his life, so he decided to put it to work. He later told a friend of his, John Francis Cassidy, that he became a loan shark. He hoarded his pay and allowances, and loaned it to other soldiers, charging interest. He was making good money. Then the Army interfered. In May 1962 he was posted to the 46th Army Surgical Hospital in Landstuhl, West Germany. His job title was Orderly.

Cassidy said Heidnik got to Germany, realized what had happened, and almost had a heart attack. He had almost $5,000 out in loans, and he had left in such a hurry he didn't have time to collect. Fat chance he had in Germany. He had to kiss that money good-bye.

Within a few weeks Heidnik took the test for his high school equivalency diploma. He did very well, scoring ninety-six percent. That was twenty-eight points above the standard. Then something really strange happened.

Three months after arriving at Landstuhl, he went on sick call. On August 25, 1962, he asked to see a doctor, saying he had dizzy spells, headaches, and blurred vision in his right eye. He was nauseated much of the time and was vomiting, he added. The doctor noted Heidnik also had a visible tic; at irregular intervals his head would jerk horizontally.

A hospital neurologist examined him and decided he was suffering from gastroenteritis. He also noted that Heidnik seemed to exhibit symptoms of a mental illness: he was either schizoid or schizophrenic.

Dr. Jack Apsche, a Philadelphia psychologist who spent months piecing together Heidnik's complicated medical records, said those initial symptoms the soldier Heidnik suffered pointed not so much toward psychosis as to the after-effects of hallucinogens. While schizophrenics are noted for emotional frigidity, aloofness, and an inability to develop close relationships, Heidnik's complaints were subtly different. He admitted he did not respond well to authority, and he also griped that others did not like him because he performed his jobs better than they did. "I was by far the best," he told one doctor, and others "pulled rank out of jealousy."

Also, when Apsche saw the drugs that were prescribed for Heidnik, an alarm went off. His medication included Stelazine, which particularly attracted Apsche's attention. It is a major tranquilizer. Not a Valium. Stelazine has K-I-C-K. "If one examines the adverse reaction of these drugs as listed in *Physicians Desk Reference,* it would be questionable why someone would be placed on these without a diagnosis of severe psychosis or some other psychiatric definition," said Apsche. "It is obvious that they are drugs of choice for someone who is hallucinating." Apsche believed the Army must have understood Heidnik's condition was serious.

On October 25, two months to the day after he reported sick, Heidnik was transferred back to the United States, to the military hospital in Valley Forge, Pennsylvania. There, in addition to his other symptoms, an attending physician said Heidnik also complained of "seeing things moving." The doctor noted this suggested an "hallucinatory experience."

This had not been recorded in his Landstuhl file although Heidnik later told Apsche he had listed it among his symptoms when he was first examined. Its absence in his initial file suggested to Apsche that it may have thrown the entire diagnosis out of kilter.

"Either Heidnik was having a psychotic reaction (vis-à-vis the hallucination) or was responding to an hallucinatory agent. Since he was not a schizoid personality type," said Apsche, "it is understandable that this diagnosis (of schizophrenia) was totally erroneous and that Heidnik was having an hallucinatory experience."

Three months later, on January 23, 1963, an Army board reviewed the diagnosis of Heidnik as someone suffering from a schizoid personality disorder and recommended he be given an honorable discharge. Heidnik protested, but it did no good. A week later he was dismissed from the service. Ultimately, he would be judged one hundred percent mentally disabled.

On January 30, 1963, without being released from the hospital, Heidnik was given an honorable discharge. He served only fourteen months of a thirty-six month enlistment. He also received a pension for a service-connected mental disability. The pension was originally ten percent, but once his papers worked their way through all the channels, it was raised to one hundred percent and made retroactive to his discharge date.

After he left the Army, Gary settled in Philadelphia. He graduated as a Licensed Practical Nurse and got his state certificate. He also enrolled at the University of Pennsylvania and earned credits in chemistry, composition, anthropology, history, sociology, biology, commercial law, and marketing.

With his ticket as an LPN, he went to work in the University of Pennsylvania hospital (from which he was later fired because of sloppy work) and started training as a psychiatric nurse at the Veterans Administration hospital in Coatesville, near Philadelphia. He never finished that course; he was booted out after about four months because of poor attendance and a bad attitude.

About that time, he decided to try to make up with Michael and his stepmother. It didn't take. He went back to Cleveland but left again before the stamp on his ticket was dry. That time it was for good. He never went back.

Gary's relationship with his mother was not much better. He said years later that one of the reasons he joined the Army was because his mother was hitting him up for money to buy booze. Over the years, they kept loosely in touch, but were never close. On May 30, 1970, Ellen Heidnik, née Rutledge, riddled with bone cancer and the effects of alcoholism, gulped her last drink: the contents of a bottle of mercuric chloride, a chemical commonly found in beauty shops. Gary had her cremated and then took her ashes to Niagara Falls, where he dumped them over the precipice.

His own destructive path was written in his stars even then. He already had a long history of admissions to mental hospitals. He would have a lot more.

Chapter 6

November 29, 1986

The next time Gary Heidnik came into the cellar, Josefina Rivera heard him before she saw him.

She was still squatting in the shallow pit, cramped beyond belief, when Heidnik thumped down the stairs. This time, though, he had someone with him—a woman who was crying and saying she didn't want to go.

"Shut up," she heard Heidnik say. "I'm not going to hurt you."

Despite the radio which was still blaring away, Rivera heard him repeating the shackling procedure with the new arrival. Finally, Heidnik came over and slid the board back. Reaching down, he grabbed her arm and pulled her up. She was so stiff she could hardly stand. She was dizzy, too, from lack of food, and the whole world seemed to be spinning. When it slowed down she looked up, straight into the eyes of a dark-skinned, pleasant-looking woman about her age. The woman's jaw hung slightly open and her eyes looked as big as saucers behind the thick lenses of her pearl-colored plastic glasses. She wasn't comprehending this at all, Rivera realized. She didn't know what was going on.

"Nicole," Heidnik said, using the only name by which he knew Rivera, "this is Sandy." Turning to the new woman: "Sandy, this is Nicole." He might have been introducing two women at an afternoon tea.

When Heidnik left, Sandy explained that her name was Sandra Lindsay and she had known Gary Heidnik for four years.

"I met him when he used to hang around Elwyn," she said, explaining painstakingly to Rivera that the Elwyn Institute was an institute for the mentally and physically handicapped which was located on Market Street, across the Schuylkill River, on the other side of town.

"Gary was good to me," she added. "He used to bring me here all the time and take me to McDonald's. We used to have a lot of fun."

"Did you ever have sex with him?" Rivera asked.

"Oh, yeah," Lindsay replied. "Him and Tony both."

"Who is Tony?" Rivera wanted to know.

"Tony Brown," said Lindsay. "A black man. A friend of Gary's. He used to drive Gary's car."

Lindsay confided that she had once been pregnant with Heidnik's baby, but the thought of being a mother frightened her so she had an abortion.

"That made Gary really mad," she said. "He criticized me at church on Sunday and said abortions were evil. Then he offered me a thousand dollars to have his baby. But I don't want to do it. Now he says I'm going to have his baby whether I want to or not."

Rivera looked carefully at Lindsay. Her skin was a deep, chocolate brown and as smooth as an infant's. She had rather large, sturdy bones and carried herself well. Basically, she seemed to be a happy person, caught up in a circumstance she could not comprehend. In fact, Lindsay, formally classified as mildly retarded, could not understand why her friend Gary had suddenly turned against her.

As Rivera watched, Lindsay took off her glasses—which was all she was wearing, except for a wrinkled blouse—and cried. They were big, deep sobs that made her whole body shake.

"Let me have your glasses," Rivera said, reaching for the spectacles. "You won't need them here." Carefully she folded the glasses and stuck them in the only place available, the ball rack on the pool table.

As Lindsay cried, Rivera thought about her own life and how it contrasted markedly from Lindsay's. Although Lindsay had a high school diploma, she had graduated through the special education program. Rivera, too, was a high school graduate, but she was the product of a tough inner-city girl's school run by Catholic nuns. While Lindsay led a protected home life, watched over as carefully as possible by a solicitous mother, Rivera had been on the streets as long as she could remember. Lindsay had had a single abortion; Rivera had three children. That part of what she had told Heidnik had been the truth. But none of the children lived with her, and she certainly had not hired a babysitter to watch them while she turned tricks.

Rivera was twenty-five years old, with the heart and cunning of a fifty-year-old; Lindsay, the same age, had as much savvy and sophistication as a fifteen-year-old.

Before Heidnik dashed back upstairs, Rivera had sensed that he was nervous about Lindsay. He should have been; his decision to bring her into the basement was a reckless one. Lindsay's family knew who he was, at least indirectly. They definitely knew Tony Brown, who was a frequent visitor in their home. And they knew of Brown's relationship with the strange white man named Gary.

Brown, despite the fact that he also was mildly retarded, could still put it together if someone from Lindsay's family went to him and asked where Sandy was likely to have disappeared.

If Heidnik was feeling uneasy, he covered it with rare

hospitality. An hour after he left them alone, he returned with a welcome chant. "It's dinner time," he said, producing a handful of crackers and a bottle of water.

Rivera looked at the meager offering and cursed herself for refusing the sandwich and juice the day before. If she had it in front of her now, she wouldn't have had any qualms about digging in. Being poisoned was probably better than starving to death. At least it was quicker.

Without another word Heidnik turned and again retreated up the stairs, leaving the women to get better acquainted. In a way, they were sort of related: two wives in a growing harem.

A few hours later Heidnik returned and resumed digging in the pit, anxious now to make it large enough for two. Again, after some vigorous digging, he stopped and went over to Lindsay. Rivera knew what was coming; she had been there already. She was quickly learning his pattern. First he forced Lindsay to take his penis in her mouth, and then he entered her in the conventional way. Then he forced Rivera to have sex with him too. Afterwards, he turned mildly talkative.

"Sandy has been promising to have one of my babies," Heidnik said, confirming what Lindsay had already said. "She keeps backing out, but this time she's going to have to go through with it."

The next morning, after preparing and serving the women a breakfast of hot oatmeal, they all were startled by a loud pounding on the front door. Heidnik raced upstairs and peeked through the shades. Outside was Sandra Lindsay's sister, Teresa Lomax, and two cousins.

He ignored their pounding and went back downstairs. "That's your sister," he told Lindsay. "She must have gotten my address from Tony."

After a few minutes the pounding stopped and the visitors went away. Heidnik went to check to make sure they were gone, and when he returned, he was carrying several blank sheets of paper and a pen.

"Write what I tell you," he commanded Lindsay, dictating slowly so she could print it.

" 'Dear Mom,' " Heidnik ordered her to scribble, " 'do not worry. I will call.' " Laboriously, Lindsay wrote it down.

"Now sign it," he ordered.

When she did, Heidnik ordered her to address an envelope. "I'm going to mail this from New York," he told her, sealing the note inside. "Then your mother will think you just ran away. She won't be coming here looking for you."

When he left, the two women looked unhappily at each other. Instinctively they knew darker days were ahead.

Chapter 7

January 1963–September 1972

Most people's lives are measured by traditional milestones: births, deaths, marriages, educational achievements, career moves, and the like. Gary Heidnik's is measured in admissions to psychiatric hospitals.

From the time he entered the Army hospital in Landstuhl in August 1962, until he was arrested in March 1987, he had been in and out of different hospitals twenty-one times. Those are documentable admissions. There is a huge six-year gap in his records that shows no hospitalizations. Given his history before and after, that is virtually impossible. He almost had to be somewhere. But no one knows where.

During that time he also attempted suicide thirteen times. Documentable. At his trial the prosecutor would scoff. They weren't *serious* attempts, he said. Not serious? Once he drove his motorcycle head-on into a truck. Another time he tried to hang himself. Once he chopped up a light bulb and gulped down the glass. Several times he tried to O.D. on Stelazine or Thorazine, his two most common medications. It was usually after such attempts that he was hospitalized, more frequently than not, voluntarily. Either he would surrender himself, or his brother Terry would take him in. Sometimes he would return the favor by taking Terry to the hospital when *he* was suicidal.

His astounding admissions record began not long after he was discharged from the Army. Within a year he tried suicide by ingesting thirty 50-milligram tablets of Thorazine, a cousin to Stelazine. That didn't work, so he tried rat poison. He had the doctors' attention.

Two psychiatrists examined him after his second attempt. One said he had an undetermined psychosis and was suffering from acute depression. The other diagnosed him as a schizophrenic.

Heidnik wasn't helping them much, since he decided to go mute. He would do this periodically for the next quarter century. Just quit talking. Sometimes he wrote notes. Sometimes he used sign language. Sometimes he just sat and stared.

This time, his silent period lasted three weeks. According to the records, when he started talking again his speech was blurred. His thoughts wandered. He was often incoherent.

While doctors were trying to decide whether to release him or hold him, he walked away. In mental-health-institution jargon it's called AMA—Against Medical Advice. Over the years he AMA'ed a lot.

A few days after he strolled off, the cops nabbed him for driving a motorcycle at night with a broken headlight. He admitted he was a mental patient and they took him back to the hospital.

Two weeks later he was released. But two nights after that, on Halloween eve, 1966, he had the head-on collision. He said he wanted to kill himself. He was only slightly injured. Then, while being treated at a regular hospital for the accident injuries, he took some Stelazine capsules he had hoarded during his previous hospitalization. His doctors sent him back to the nut ward.

This time he was placed on suicide watch and examined more thoroughly. The judgment was by now becoming familiar: Heidnik was diagnosed as suffering a schizophrenic reaction and an anxiety reaction. He also was found to be a catatonic type. When a series of intelligence tests were given him, he scored in the ninety-fifth percentile of the entire adult population. The record noted "a score at this level is classified as superior, and even when compared with college students, his score surpassed seventy-five percent of them."

There was one other finding that was significant, especially when viewed in light of what would occur later. Another test revealed that Heidnik desperately needed to be in a position of authority.

After that, Heidnik's hospitalizations tumbled one atop the other. By then, too, a pattern was developing. The nurses had to watch him or he wouldn't take his medicine. He'd hoard it for a killer cocktail. Mutism also became a Heidnik trademark. In February 1968 he walked into the VA hospital in Coatesville but refused to speak. A nurse asked him to remove his watch. He ripped it off, threw it on the floor and stomped on it. When he undressed for the physical, doctors found a string tied tightly around one toe. What was that for? Heidnik scribbled a note saying he wanted to induce gangrene, which he hoped would spread throughout his system and kill him.

In December 1968 he was readmitted again after he hit his brother Terry over the head with a wood plane.

As Terry lay in his hospital bed recuperating from the blow, Gary walked through the door.

Terry looked up, surprised to see his brother. "What if you had killed me?" he asked angrily.

Gary looked down at him and waited a long time to answer.

"I would have put your body in the bathtub and poured acid over it to dissolve the bones," he finally said. "I would have had to be careful while mixing the acid, though, because I wouldn't want to damage the drain-pipes. I would leave you there to soak for two or three days, and if there were any big bones left, I'd saw them up and put them in a trash compactor. Then I'd dis-tribute them around the neighborhood in various trash cans."

Terry was speechless. For a long time after that, he said, he had nightmares in which Gary would be chasing him with a wood plane.

For almost two years Gary was hospital free. Then he was back, complaining of depression over his mother's suicide. Since she killed herself by taking a fatal dose of mercuric poison, Heidnik refused medication containing a mercury derivative.

Doctors decided to give him a little test. They asked him to make up two stories. One of his tales was a sym-bolic one. It represented the passage from darkness to light, or, psychologically interpreted, from depression to a more optimistic outlook. The second story was more like a brief essay. It was a story about a religious fanatic who jumped out a window. His last words were, "God, here I come."

Which of those tales more closely represent your views? the doctors asked. "The abstract one," Heidnik replied. How about the other one? "I'm not very reli-gious," he told the doctor. This later became significant.

Also listed in the record at this time was the fact that the day before he was admitted, his live-in girlfriend walked out on him. At the time, he was twenty-seven years old. His girlfriend was a decade or so older, a men-tally retarded black woman who had spent almost one third of her life in mental institutions.

In 1971 he added another eccentricity to his growing personal list. It was summer. It was hot. He showed up at a VA hospital in Maryland wearing a black-leather motorcycle jacket. He refused to take it off. And he refused to talk.

Silently, he bent over and rolled up his right pants leg. "When I do that," he wrote, "it means I don't want to be bothered."

By this time some of his psychiatrists were beginning to wonder if he was going to be around forever. "The patient seems to be settling in for life," one doctor wrote in his chart.

In August he invented another trademark: a snappy military salute. The interesting thing about these eccentricities is they would follow him over the years. Once adopted, never forgotten. The salute. The mutism. The disregard for hygiene. Heidnikisms all. One doctor with a way with words later inscribed for posterity his opinion of Heidnik's bathing habits. "He is quite unkempt in appearance and . . . is still wearing the same leather jacket [which is] creating a social disturbance through its odoriferous emanations."

Another psychiatrist described him as "a residual schizophrenic" with lack of motivation or initiative and a "disregard for the usual customs, both social and cultural."

It was about this time, Apsche feels, that Heidnik began seeing himself in a separate world governed by his own sense of morality. "This," he said, "was Heidnik reality."

On September 19, 1972, Gary Heidnik was discharged from another hospital. This is notable only because it marked the beginning of an inexplicable hole in his record. There is nothing else until 1978. To Jack Apsche this does not mean that Heidnik's mental problems were in some sort of remission. He could have gone to a hospital in another state or he could have been in a private hospital. One thing can be assumed with confidence, Apsche said: Heidnik was not getting any better.

"It is apparent that there were precursors and predictions, maybe even prophecies, of what was going to transpire," said Apsche. "Every sign of extreme psychosis was in operation. Here was a man with no control, screaming for help, but no one listened. He had delusions, hallucinations, both auditory and visual; he had attempted suicide and he was suffering from extreme depression. Here was a man who had lost touch with reality. There were many clear warning signs that this man was heading for a total psychotic suicidal or homicidal experience."

When Heidnik came to trial, the defense attorney called Apsche as a witness. However, the bulk of the psychologist's material detailing Heidnik's convoluted hospital history never got before the jury. In an unusual move, the judge ruled that Apsche could not go into detail. He could talk about dates, medicine, and symptoms, but not about diagnoses. This was a boon for the prosecution. Without the defense being able to proffer a pattern of medical opinions, the prosecutor argued loudly and apparently convincingly that Heidnik had been faking mental illness for twenty-five years. His alleged motive: some $2,000 a month in benefits from the Veterans Administration and the Social Security Administration.

Chapter 8

Summer and Fall, 1971

That $2,000 a month, though, was paltry compared to what he could collect from another sure-fire money-maker: a church.

In the spring of 1971 Gary Heidnik, who had never before professed any strong religious leanings, opened a dialogue with God. One morning he walked out of his Philadelphia apartment and climbed into his battered Plymouth. He planned, he said, to drive down the street for coffee and a doughnut. He headed west. When he got to the Pacific Ocean he stopped. Standing in the surf at Malibu, gazing at the sunset, Gary Heidnik said he was visited by the Almighty. He told Heidnik to go back to Philadelphia and start a new church. Someone needed to care for the mentally and physically handicapped. Years later he would say he also conversed from time to time with Jesus. Jesus gave him stock-market tips.

A few months after the California trip, while he was under treatment at one of the mental hospitals, he applied to incorporate the United Church of the Ministers of God. The application was approved on October 12, 1971. Founding members included his brother Terry, a retarded woman he was living with at the time, and a handful of other people. Attached to the application was a raggedly typed five-page "constitution" setting forth the church structure and principles.

The document mandated the selection of a five-member board of directors. It would select a "bishop" who would rule "for life or until the so selected chooses to resign." Overnight, ex-private Gary Heidnik became Bishop Gary Heidnik.

The bishop had "full control and responsibility for church funds." He also had the power to determine how these funds would be raised. Among the suggested avenues were "loans, stocks, bingo games, business ventures, and other endeavors."

In 1975 Bishop Heidnik plunked down $1,500 and opened an account in the church's name with Merrill Lynch, Pierce, Fenner & Smith. Since he was a child he had been obsessed with Wall Street. Now he could play it for real. Over the next twelve years, no matter which hospital he was in or where he went, Bishop Heidnik always made sure that Merrill Lynch's monthly financial statements got to him. He also kept in close touch with his broker. Over the years that $1,500 mushroomed into a $545,000 portfolio.

His broker would later testify that Bishop Heidnik's game plan was solid. "He was," he admitted, "an astute investor." Astute but not perfect. He had one weakness. In a child-support hearing years later, Heidnik would appear embarrassed about his one not-so-wise investment. "I just couldn't resist Crazy Eddie," he confessed, a stock whose value plummeted soon after Heidnik invested $158,000.

The "constitution" also spelled out how the church funds would be dispersed. Assets, it said, would be used "for furthering the goals of the church, such as purchase of buildings for worship, administration, education, and heat, etc." This apparently included motor vehicles, too, since his fleet was church-listed.

Over the following months the genuineness of the church would become a highly debatable issue. One school argued that it was a blatant strategy to evade taxes. Another asserted just as sincerely that it was a humanitarian association.

If it was a con game, however, it was an elaborate one.

The "constitution" covered religious as well as secular matters and was quite specific on points of ecclesiastical doctrine. It defined the Bible, preferably the New World version, as the "guiding inspiration." However, it also noted, "it is to be remembered that it is only an interpretation of the original Scriptures."

"The divinity of Christ is questionable," the document continued, "but He is recognized as God's prophet and our savior, hence his claim of Divine Origin is to be played down."

As with secular issues, the "constitution" gave virtually unlimited power to the bishop: "His is the final word on interpretation of the Bible or the settling of religious disputes." There was one exception: "divine intervention."

When he wasn't in the hospital, Bishop Heidnik regularly held "services" wherever he happened to be living. Early on Sunday, Tony Brown would climb behind the wheel of the most commodious vehicle then owned by the church and make the rounds, picking up congregants. Since many of them couldn't read, Heidnik would painstakingly teach them the words to hymns and crank up his stereo to play recorded gospel music. Usually he would preach a short sermon. Then they would pile back into the car and Heidnik would take them all to lunch at McDonald's or Roy Rogers. Sometimes they would go to a theme park in New Jersey or some other recreational spot.

Those who saw the "church" in operation swore to its authenticity. Heidnik's friend, John Francis Cassidy, said he walked into Heidnik's house one Sunday morning and found twenty people standing around, singing hymns. He was impressed. "Up until then, I always thought it was a dodge," he said.

By 1986, fifteen years after it began, the church was not only thriving, but wealthy. Within two years of that, a long list of people would be fighting over its funds, including the U.S. government's Peace Corps. Heidnik himself inadvertently brought the federal agency into the battle through the will-like last paragraph in the "constitution."

"If and when dissolution [of the church] should ever become necessary," it said, "the total assets of the church should be given directly or sold and the profits given equally to the federal government's Peace Corps and Veterans Administration."

Chapter 9

For Sandra Lindsay and Josefina Rivera, life in Gary Heidnik's dingy cellar settled into a nightmarish routine. They adjusted as best they could, but it wasn't easy, considering the grim surroundings: the bare, littered floor, the empty walls, a constantly blaring radio, and an overhead light that never went off; the cold, the damp—the sheer indignity of it all.

Since the only article of clothing they were allowed to wear was a thin shirt, they often huddled together for warmth and pleaded for blankets and more clothing. Even worse was the lack of contact with the outside world, the constant sexual demands by their captor, the ever-present threat of being beaten, and—always present —the hunger. Heidnik fed them little, and what he did give them was hardly appetizing. Occasionally he served them oatmeal for breakfast, but usually it was Pop-Tarts, crackers, and white bread. Dinner was rice and shriveled hot dogs, and for special treats, takeout fried chicken.

The two women were totally subject to Heidnik's sexual whims, which were more patterned than bizarre. He preferred the first contact to be oral-genital, but he did not want to climax in their mouths. His aim was not sexual gratification but a single-minded desire to get them pregnant. Every day, at least once a day, he would visit them in the basement and demand sex from one or both of them. They didn't even think of refusing.

Heidnik warned them over and over not to scream, not to yell, not to do anything that would alert anyone to their presence. His threats were not always heeded. When Heidnik took to beating them, Rivera and Lindsay howled and shrieked, cursing and begging for mercy. That usually made Heidnik beat them harder.

He wasn't particularly worried about the neighbors taking notice, but just in case, he tacked soundproofing material to the ceiling to help deaden any noise they might make. But the best remedy was to convince them not to make any noise at all. If they did, he beat them with a shovel handle. Or he put them in the pit, "the hole," and covered it with a board and put sandbags on top. Then he would feed them only bread and water or nothing at all for a day or two. Or he used the stretch punishment.

Soon after he brought them into the cellar, he screwed a large eye hook into a ceiling beam so it would be about seven feet off the floor. If one of them misbehaved, he would put a handcuff on one wrist and the matching cuff through the eye hook. The woman being punished would then have to stand, for hours on end, with one arm above her head, unable to lie down, sit, or shift positions.

These punishments and precautions were necessary, he told them, because there was a constant danger they would be discovered and his plan would be wrecked. Lindsay's relatives were still coming by and banging on his door, so the letter he made her write in an attempt to convince them she was not in his house had been only partly successful, even when he followed it up with a Christmas card early in December and enclosed a five dollar bill.

While the correspondence may not have done much to discourage Lindsay's family, it apparently did have the desired effect on the police. Lindsay's mother reported her missing the Monday after the Saturday she left home. The case was assigned to Sergeant Julius Armstrong, a black officer with seventeen years in the department. She told him that she suspected her daughter might be a prisoner of a man named Gary who lived in a house at 3520 North Marshall Street. She even gave him a telephone number. The only thing she did not know was Gary's last name.

Like Lindsay's sister, Sergeant Armstrong came by and beat on Heidnik's door. Like her, he got no response. He dialed the number. No one answered. So he went looking for Tony Brown, the contact between Lindsay and Heidnik. He found him at a McDonald's in West Philadelphia, a popular hangout for Heidnik and his retarded friends from the Elwyn Institute.

"What is Gary's last name?" Armstrong asked Brown.

"Heidnik," said Brown.

"How do you spell that?" Armstrong wanted to know.

Brown thought about it. "H-E-I-D-A-I-K-E," he answered.

Armstrong wrote it down in his pad.

Later, back at his district headquarters, Armstrong punched the name Brown had spelled for him into the computer. The search produced nothing.

By this time Lindsay's mother had received the letter. She took it to Armstrong. Ah-ha, thought the cop, Lindsay is a twenty-five-year-old runaway, not a kidnap victim. Although he didn't stop working on the case altogether, he admitted in his testimony later that after he was shown the letter and the card, he did not give it a high priority. Under cross-examination by Heidnik's lawyer, Armstrong confessed he made no concerted attempt to identify Gary, not even following through on such basic procedures as checking the tax rolls or utility records to find the surname of the man who lived at 3520 North Marshall. His sole source for the identification had been a mentally deficient man.

If he had followed through and learned that the Marshall Street Gary was Gary Heidnik, and then if he had punched H-E-I-D-N-I-K into the computer, the result would have sent him running to his patrol car. He could have discovered, by pressing a few keys, that a half-dozen years previously, Gary Heidnik had done time for kidnapping a retarded black woman and hiding her in a basement storage bin. That information might have saved two lives.

Chapter 10

The computer, in fact, would have spit out more than one mention of Gary Heidnik. He may have been better known on the mental-health circuit, but he was certainly no stranger to the Philadelphia Police Department. He had an arrest record going back to 1976, when he was charged with aggravated assault, carrying a pistol without a license, and carrying a firearm on the public streets.

The charges stemmed from an incident involving a black man named Robert Rogers. Rogers' then-girlfriend, later to be his wife, was renting an apartment from Heidnik, who at the time owned a dilapidated three-story house on Cedar Avenue in a run-down neighborhood in West Philadelphia, not far from the University of Pennsylvania.

Heidnik and Rogers' girlfriend had an argument, so Heidnik went into the basement and turned off all the electricity in the building. When Rogers came home, the woman told him what had happened, and he went to the cellar to turn the power back on. When he got to the basement door, however, it was locked. So he went outside, opened a cellar window and climbed in. Inside, sitting on the floor on a baby mattress, was Heidnik. He had a rifle in his hands. When Rogers came in, Heidnik put the rifle down and picked up a pistol.

"I got you and I'm going to kill you and say you're a burglar," Heidnik said, lifting the pistol, aiming it at Rogers' face and pulling the trigger. Rogers turned his head just in time. The bullet grazed his cheek.

"I kind of talked him out of shooting me a second time," Rogers recalled. "We went outside, and when the police came up, I snatched his gun and struck him."

The charges were dismissed a week later. The record does not say why.

Not long after the incident, Heidnik sold the house to a University of Pennsylvania administrator, who was interested not so much in the property as in getting Heidnik out of the neighborhood. When the man and his wife started cleaning up the building, they found it littered with pornography and garbage.

Even more disturbing, they found a place in the basement where Heidnik had chopped a hole about two-feet square through the concrete, then scooped out the dirt under the slab to create a pit large enough to hold an adult. Did Heidnik dig the hole to hide in? To climb into to protect himself? Or as a cell for a captive?

If his behavior in the fall of 1976 failed to elicit much notice from law enforcement officials, Heidnik certainly got their attention twenty months later.

After he vacated the Cedar Avenue house, he moved in with Anjeanette Davidson, a retarded black woman who had an apartment at 2331 North Fifty-eighth Street—another poor Philadelphia neighborhood.

While not feebleminded enough to require institutionalization, Anjeanette was unable to read or write. Later, a psychiatrist would gauge her IQ at 49. (Heidnik, tested at the same time, scored 130.) Generally, a score of 100 is recognized as average, and 70 is the cutoff point to certify retardation. A score of 130 is considered superior.

Anjeanette got pregnant, but Heidnik, who had a certificate as an LPN, insisted on treating her at home and refused to allow her to receive outside medical attention. A month before the baby was due, Anjeanette's older sister went to the apartment with a police escort and took Anjeanette away. A medical examination disclosed she had a large fibroid tumor that would have prevented a normal delivery. On March 22, 1978, she delivered, by Caesarean section, a seven-pound, eight-ounce girl. Because of Heidnik's strict eating regimen, Anjeanette had gained only five pounds during her pregnancy. As soon as the baby girl was born, she was put in a foster home.

A few weeks later, on May 7, Heidnik and Anjeanette drove to Selinsgrove Center, an institution for the mentally retarded near Harrisburg, in central Pennsylvania, to visit Anjeanette's sister Alberta.

With an IQ of only 30—roughly the mental capacity of a five-year-old—Alberta could not read, write, or distinguish between coins. She could, however, feed, clothe, and clean herself. Then thirty-four, she had been in the center since she was fourteen.

The two sisters were delighted to see each other. While they chatted happily in a corner, Heidnik filled out a pass signing her out of the institution for a short-term visit. The time was twelve-thirty, and Heidnik promised to return her to the center by the next morning at the latest. They never came back.

When Alberta had not returned by May 16, center officials secured a court order demanding her return. But first they had to find her. The first stop was Heidnik's and Anjeanette's apartment in Philadelphia.

Heidnik answered the door and told the woman from the center that Alberta was not there. If she did not believe him, he added, swinging the door wide, she could come in and look for herself. The woman walked through the apartment and did not find Alberta.

"Where is she?" she demanded.

"I put her on a bus back to Selinsgrove," Heidnik replied.

Reluctantly, the woman left.

By the next day, when Alberta still had not returned, center officials were getting frantic. The woman who had been to Heidnik's the day before went back, but on the way she stopped to pick up a police escort.

Again Heidnik told her Alberta was not there, and again she went through the apartment without finding Alberta. This time, though, they decided to search the entire building.

They found Alberta cowering in an unused storage room in the basement. When Alberta saw the woman from the center, she ran to her and hugged her tightly. She was trembling violently.

"Let's go," the woman said. "We're going home."

"Wait a minute," interjected Heidnik. "If you go with them," he told Alberta, "they're going to lock you up and you'll never see your sister again." She went anyway.

Once back at the center, Alberta was given a thorough physical. Doctors discovered a tear on the vestibule of her vagina, which indicated recent intercourse. Even more upsetting to center officials, a chemical test showed traces of sperm in her mouth and gonorrhea in her throat, a condition that could result only from oral-genital sex.

Three weeks later, at the center's urging, police returned to Heidnik's apartment. This time they arrested him and charged him with kidnapping, rape, false imprisonment, unlawful restraint, involuntary deviate sexual intercourse, interfering with the custody of a committed person, and recklessly endangering another person. He pleaded innocent.

His defense seemed off to a good start when he agreed to submit to a test for venereal disease. It was negative, meaning Heidnik did not have gonorrhea. Not at that time anyway.

Chapter 11

November 1978–March 1983

Surprisingly, when the case came to trial the following November, Heidnik took the stand.

"When we left the center on May seventh," he swore, "we went to a restaurant named Gary's, where we stayed for an hour and a half. From there we went to get ice cream at a Dairy Queen. Then, when we were driving Alberta back to the center, she started crying. She said she wanted to be with her sister, so we brought her back to Philadelphia."

The next day, Heidnik testified, he telephoned the center and asked officials to list Alberta as being on vacation so she could stay longer. He said the request was tentatively approved.

That night, he said, he went to work, and when he came home the next morning, Anjeanette and Alberta were crying and upset.

"What happened?" he asked. "What's the matter?"

Anjeanette told him the center had telephoned and said Alberta had to come back.

Instead of returning her to the center, Heidnik said, they took her shopping and bought her two dresses, a purse, an inexpensive watch, and a wig. Over the next few days, he said, he treated calluses on her hands and feet and worked with her to help her learn how to handle money. He hid her, he admitted, because she said she did not want to go back to the center. He thought he was helping her. He denied keeping her captive or forcing her to have sex with him.

Under cross-examination Heidnik was forced into admissions that damaged his credibility. For one thing, although he had tested negative on a VD test, he admitted that he had access to antibiotics that he could have taken to cure the disease. He also admitted lying to Selinsgrove officials about Alberta's whereabouts.

As a mitigating circumstance, he said he was being treated for schizophrenia.

Since he had waived a jury trial, the decision on his fate was left to Common Pleas Court Judge Charles P. Mirarchi Jr., an owlish-looking veteran on the criminal circuit who had heard a lot of wild tales in his time. As far as he was concerned, this story of Heidnik's was one of the wildest tales he'd heard yet. The judge's instincts told him Heidnik was big trouble, especially with a psychiatric report in hand that said that even with an IQ of 130 Heidnik was a mental basket case.

"He appears to be an extremely insecure and confused individual," the report said. "Records indicate he is suffering from a major mental illness, which apparently has been of long standing. He is also psychosexually immature. He appears to be easily threatened by women whom he would consider to be equal to him either intellectually or emotionally. His defense cannot tolerate criticism. Gary needs constant acceptance and self-assurance that he is an intelligent, worthwhile human being."

Mirarchi found Heidnik guilty, but ordered the standard presentence report done. It was even more foreboding.

"Heidnik appears to be manipulative, and he is certainly lacking in judgment," wrote Joseph A. Tobin, the presentence criminal investigator. "He impresses me as one who sees himself as superior to others, although apparently he must involve himself with those distinctly inferior to himself to reinforce this. . . . It is my opinion, based on my extensive investigation, that he is not only a danger to himself, but perhaps a greater danger to others in the community, especially those who he perceives as being weak and dependent. Unfortunately, it seems to me that he will not significantly change his aberrant behavior pattern in the near future."

That was enough for Mirarchi. He gave Heidnik as stiff a sentence as he could, considering that the felony charges—rape, kidnapping, false imprisonment, and involuntary deviate sexual intercourse—had to be dropped because they could not be prosecuted without Alberta's testimony. She was judged too retarded to take the stand. What Mirarchi was left with was a handful of misdemeanors: recklessly endangering another person, interfering with the custody of a committed person, and unlawful restraint. It was enough. He sentenced Heidnik to three to seven years in the state penitentiary.

"If it had been within my power to give him longer, I would have," Mirarchi said ten years later. At the time, long before Heidnik's name would be in headlines, Mirarchi sensed something sinister about Heidnik, "something evil and dangerous."

Heidnik's attorney, however, thought the sentence was severe and pleaded for leniency, arguing that Heidnik had no prior convictions, that he had not been accused of committing a violent crime, and that no weapons were involved. "It is a crime which would lead a court, in my opinion, to believe that he is not dangerous to society."

Mirarchi ordered still another report. This one, from court psychiatrist Dr. Wayne C. Blodgett, was the harshest yet, one which, a decade later, would look like a crystal-ball prophecy.

Blodgett predicted there was a "high probability" Heidnik would commit similar crimes in the future. "Of particular concern," he wrote, "is the defendant's potential for engaging in sexually assaultive crimes against females. In order to avoid such a tragedy in the future, it will be necessary for him to be very closely supervised and for him to receive continuing surveillance over a long period of time."

As it turned out, the time was not long enough.

Heidnik, who already frequently referred to himself as "bishop," now took on a third identity: he became prisoner number F-9748. Despite his new persona, however, he never did a day of hard time. Instead, he spent the next four years, two months, and fourteen days bouncing from one state hospital to the other. He went from the facility at Graterford Prison to Norristown State Hospital to the maximum-security hospital for the criminally insane at Farview and back to start the circle all over again. Over the course of his prison time, Heidnik was transferred from one hospital to another at least a half-dozen times.

Halfway through the sentence, he went mute. He simply quit talking. As he had done in the VA hospital, he rolled up one pants leg and wrote a note saying it was a signal that no one was to talk to him. When asked why he wouldn't talk, Heidnik scribbled a note saying the Devil had shoved a cookie down his throat.

One doctor told him to open wide and say aaahh. After a quick look with a flashlight, he told Heidnik he couldn't see any cookie. Heidnik scribbled another note: "Pray for eyes."

The mute period continued, with only brief relief, for the next two-and-a-half years. One of the exceptions occurred during a visit from his old friend, John Francis Cassidy. When the two met, Heidnik started chatting away as though nothing was amiss.

The guard, who had known only the silent Heidnik, almost fainted. "Hey! He's talking," he exclaimed.

Heidnik flashed him a cutting glance. "Yeah, it must be a miracle," he said drily.

The parole board, though, did not see any humor in Heidnik's case. Three times he came up for parole and three times the board decided he needed more psychiatric help. Once he wrote a note to the board and signed it not G. M. Heidnik, but "G. M. Kill."

Finally, on March 24, 1983, near the end of his sentence, he was considered eligible for release. His parole, however, was dependent on his being accepted into the in-patient program at Coatesville, the VA mental unit. Some three weeks later, on April 12, he was freed, but he had to remain under state supervision for another three years. It had no effect on his future behavior.

Chapter 12

December 22, 1986

Gary Heidnik got his Christmas present early.

He was cruising the north side in his Cadillac on Monday afternoon, three days before Christmas, when he spotted a saucy-looking young woman bopping down Lehigh Street. It was a pert nineteen-year-old named Lisa Thomas, who was sashaying along in jeans and a blue thigh-length down jacket. Thomas had dropped out of high school in the eleventh grade because she was pregnant. She later had a child, and currently the two of them were living at home with Lisa's mother. They subsisted on welfare payments.

Heidnik let the Cadillac drift to a stop beside Thomas, rolled down the window and asked her a question: "You want to see my peter?"

Thomas was offended. "I'm no prostitute," she said angrily.

Heidnik apologized and asked if she wanted a ride.

"No," she said, still angry. "I'm only going to my girlfriend's house."

"Where's that?"

"Just around the corner."

"Why don't you get in and I'll take you there. I'm not going to hurt you."

Lisa looked at the handsome car. She took another

look at the driver, who had changed his tune now that she had told him she wasn't a hooker. He didn't look mean. There's no danger in accepting a ride, she thought.

Heidnik took her to her friend's and said he'd wait for her. Lisa went in, retrieved a pair of gloves she had forgotten on an earlier visit, and glanced out the window. Heidnik and his Cadillac were waiting at the curb.

"Look at that car," she bragged to her friend.

Lisa was back in a flash.

"Let's go get something to eat," Heidnik suggested.

"Okay," she agreed.

Heidnik favored McDonald's and Roy Rogers, but he apparently was anxious to impress this new woman, a dark-skinned, fresh-looking teenager with a bright smile and an adventurous spirit. He took her to a TGI Friday's.

While she was devouring a cheeseburger and fries, Heidnik asked her if she would go with him the next day to Atlantic City.

"I don't have anything to wear," she said.

"We can fix that," Heidnik said, reaching into a stuffed wallet and extracting a fifty dollar bill.

She looked at it suspiciously.

"It's for new clothes," explained Heidnik. "When you finish eating we'll go over to Sears and you can use this to buy whatever you want."

She bought two pairs of jeans and two tops. Then Heidnik asked her if he could put them on her.

She shrugged. "Okay."

Heidnik took her to North Marshall Street, gave her a wine cooler, told her to make herself comfortable. While she pulled at the drink he popped a cassette of "Splash" into the VCR.

The drink did it for Lisa Thomas. At the restaurant she had taken an allergy pill, and it was just starting to kick in. With the wine, she got so drowsy she couldn't hold her head up. In a few minutes she was sound asleep, sprawled in front of the VCR.

When she awoke sometime later, she discovered Heidnik had undressed her. She was completely nude. Heidnik carried her upstairs, put her on the waterbed, and they had sex.

Lisa got up and reached for her clothes. "Will you take me back to my girlfriend's house?" she asked.

In reply, Heidnik wrapped an arm around her throat and squeezed. She started seeing stars.

"Wait a minute," she cried. "Wait a minute. Quit choking me and I'll do whatever you want." He clapped a pair of cuffs on her wrists and pushed her down the stairs.

When she entered the basement, Lisa was still groggy and confused. She looked around and saw an empty room littered with white plastic bags.

"It's body parts in those bags, isn't it?" she asked shrilly.

"No," Heidnik answered.

"You're going to kill me. You want to kill me."

"No, I'm not going to kill you. Trust me. I'm not going to kill you."

Heidnik pointed to the board covering the pit in which Rivera and Lindsay were cowering.

"I'm going to introduce you to my two friends down here," he said.

"They're dead down there, aren't they?" Thomas screamed. "Aren't they?"

"No," Heidnik said. "But if you don't shut up, I'm going to hurt you."

He moved the board, and a half-nude woman climbed out. As Lisa watched in total amazement, the first woman was followed by another, also nude from the waist down.

"I'm Nicole," said the slimmer, lighter-colored one.

"I'm Sandy," said the other, who seemed a little dim.

Heidnik stood by beaming. Like a happy host, he produced peanut butter and jelly and started to make sandwiches. But before anyone could eat, there was a ritual that had to be completed.

Turning to Lisa, Heidnik gave her a quiet command, intent on establishing his authority. "Kiss my behind," he said.

She did.

"Who's the boss?" Heidnik asked.

"You are," she replied.

He looked at her again. "Suck my balls."

She complied.

"Suck my peter."

She did that too.

Then he forced her to have intercourse with him.

After that they ate their sandwiches and Heidnik left Thomas alone with Rivera and Lindsay.

Chapter 13

For all of his adult life, Gary Heidnik's women were almost exclusively black. This undoubtedly went back to his childhood, when his mother, whose last two husbands were black, told Gary that he was of mixed race. If he was, it certainly didn't show. His skin was milky white and his eyes as pale as ice that had been in the freezer too long. Despite what the mirror told him, he apparently thought otherwise. Later, on two separate occasions when he entered mental hospitals, he listed his race as "colored." He did not like the term black.

After he got out of the Army he invited a married black woman to come live with him. She did. They had a baby girl, but not long afterwards the woman went back to her husband and took the child with her. That was in the mid-sixties.

After that, another black woman, named Dorothy, came to live with him. She stayed around for a long time, a decade or so, until one day she simply disappeared.

Dorothy was almost a dozen years older than Heidnik and, from all accounts, mentally handicapped. She had lived in institutions for fourteen years by the time he met her, and showed signs of deep neglect. Sometime over those years her teeth had disappeared one by one. By the time she moved in with Heidnik she was, as dentists say, edentulous. She had no choppers.

Linda Rogers, the tenant who had married the man Heidnik shot in his basement in 1976, said Heidnik treated Dorothy very badly at times, yelling at her, criticizing her, occasionally beating her. When he really wanted to punish her, though, he refused to give her food. At such times she would knock on Linda's door and Linda would take her in and feed her.

Linda was a nurse, and one day Dorothy came to her and showed her a gash on her shin. It was a gunshot wound. How in the world did that happen? Linda wanted to know. Dorothy said Gary had accidentally shot her. Linda didn't say anything; she knew Heidnik kept several guns in his apartment.

When Dorothy disappeared, Heidnik seemed very worried. He said he feared she had wandered off and was unable to find her way back. A few years later, when his friend John Francis Cassidy came to visit him in prison, Heidnik told him he had seen a television documentary on street people and he thought one of the women in the film was Dorothy. He wanted to hire Cassidy to find her. Cassidy declined. "I'm not a detective," he told Heidnik.

After an exhaustive search, the police eventually found Dorothy "alive and well" but mentally more confused than ever.

Heidnik's next long-term relationship, after Dorothy, was Anjeanette. When he got out of prison he tried to find her but was unsuccessful. He couldn't figure out where she had gone.

Later, police would wonder too. They were unable to trace Anjeanette. Some investigators think Heidnik killed her and buried her in some grave they have not yet found.

Up until the time he left prison, Heidnik's batting average with long-term relationships was not too good. His

first serious lover left him and took their daughter. Dorothy, although she bore him no children, also left. And
now he couldn't find Anjeanette, although he knew exactly where his daughter was and occasionally visited
her. In the summer of 1986 his visitation rights would be
terminated despite his efforts to prevent it.

Between the spring of 1983, when he got out of prison
at age forty, and the fall of 1985 he had no single mate.
There was a white woman who was practically always at
the Marshall Street house, but she shared Tony Brown's
bed as well as Heidnik's. She later had a son which she
said was Heidnik's, and indeed was named after Heidnik.
He always referred to the boy as "Little Gary."

The child went into a foster home, too, and she began
seeing more of Tony Brown than she did of Heidnik.
Eventually she married Brown and they had a child.

But she was just one of the women having a sexual
relationship with Heidnik at the time. Another was
Jewel, a black woman of Heidnik's age. He had met Jewel
when they were both LPNs at a hospital in Philadelphia
in the sixties, and they had been lovers ever since.

The relationship developed a degree of regularity after
Heidnik got out of prison. Every other Saturday for almost two years Heidnik would pick her up, take her to
North Marshall Street, and she would spend the night.
On Sunday she would attend Heidnik's "church services," then go out to eat with the congregants. After
that, Heidnik would take her back home.

When she first met Heidnik, she said, when she was
younger, he used to tell her what a "fine specimen" of a
woman she was and how he wanted her to bear him a
son. When she made it clear she didn't want to have any
more children, he eased off.

But his sex habits also got kinkier.

"When I would go to the house, Gary would want to
make love with two women at the same time," one of his
former girlfriends told police. "I always wanted to be the

first because I didn't want him to have sex with another woman and then put his penis in me. So I would have sex with Gary, and he would like to have another woman in the bed and would bite on her breast. Then Gary would have sex with the other woman and bite my breast.".

One of the other women who participated in these activities claimed to have had Heidnik's child. Another was a friend of Heidnik's from the Elwyn Institute. Her name was Sandra Lindsay.

Early in 1987 Heidnik varied his Saturday routine with Jewel and changed the rendezvous day to Wednesday. He would pick her up at noon, take her to his house, and they would make love in the waterbed. About five P.M. they would get dressed, go get something to eat, and Heidnik would take her home.

This routine continued during almost the entire time Heidnik was holding women captive in the basement and demanding sex from them on a daily basis.

One Wednesday, said Jewel, Heidnik brought another woman with him when he came to pick her up. To Jewel, the woman looked like a Puerto Rican. She said her name was Nicole.

"She seemed to be a sweet girl," Jewel said.

The three of them lunched at Wendy's, did some shopping for Nicole in a thrift store, then went to North Marshall Street. When they got there, she and Heidnik went upstairs for their midweek sexual tryst and Nicole stayed downstairs. When they came down later, Nicole was sitting alone in the kitchen, said Jewel.

A white woman a few years younger than Heidnik said she also met Gary in the sixties, at the hospital, although she was a patient, not a member of the staff. Over the years she had a sexual relationship both with Heidnik and with Tony Brown. Once, she said, she had sex with Heidnik in the back of his van when it was parked near the Elwyn Institute as a convenient bedroom-on-wheels for whatever conquests he could make at the institution.

A black hooker told police she lived in a room at North Marshall Street off and on for several weeks in 1986. During that time, she said, the place was like a zoo.

Tony Brown and a retarded black woman, who also had a physical handicap, were living there in addition to a parade of other women who came and went. Sandra Lindsay was one. ("She would spend the night once in a while.") Also there was a black girl ("she would have epileptic seizures all the time"), a "real skinny woman from Elwyn" who was severely retarded ("she had three kids to look after and couldn't count or dial a tele- phone"), and an obese white woman who "looked like a bag lady," said the black hooker. "Gary never messed with her."

In contrast to what a former girlfriend said about Heidnik's penchant for active sex, the black hooker said around her he was entirely different. When they were in bed, she said, "Gary just wanted me to lay there and not move."

In 1983 Heidnik decided to expand his sexual-racial repertoire. While he clearly preferred blacks to whites, he decided to look east as well. He went to a matrimonial bureau and directed them to find him an Oriental virgin.

Chapter 14

January 1-18, 1987

Ten days after adding Lisa Thomas to his horror harem, Gary Heidnik went on the prowl again. This time he came home with another black woman, a twenty-three-year-old named Deborah Johnson Dudley.

How or where Heidnik picked up Dudley is still a mystery. One thing is known, however: she was a constant thorn in his side. Almost from the time he took her to join the others in the basement, she proved to be a never-ending source of aggravation.

Disharmony was already surfacing among the captives, and more dissension was not what Heidnik wanted, especially not from a woman who challenged his authority at every opportunity.

As the number of women grew, a pecking order developed. Rivera, the most streetwise of the group, was learning how to manipulate the manipulator. As time went on, Rivera was punished less frequently than the others and worked herself steadily into Heidnik's trust. Lisa Thomas, who had been abducted on December 22—the third member of the group—said she never saw Heidnik beat Rivera, although the others were regularly thrashed.

One of Heidnik's favorite tactics was to pick one of the group to be in charge when he left them alone, a sort of officer-of-the-day approach. Later he would come back

and ask the one who had been responsible who had misbehaved so he could dole out punishment. Discipline usually consisted of being whacked with the shovel handle,
but it could also include a restricted diet, time in "the
hole," or being handcuffed to the eye hook. If the one in
charge said no one had misbehaved, Heidnik punished
her.

Frequently, too, he made them beat each other, and if
the one administering the punishment was not doing it
vigorously enough, he would reverse the roles. Or he
would take over himself.

His sexual appetite showed no sign of declining. It was
a rare day when he didn't force at least one of them to
have sex with him. Sometimes he would go from one to
the other, like a bee pollinating a flower bed, until he
finally climaxed or grew tired. Later, too, according to
Thomas, he made the women, under threat of death,
have sex with each other while he watched.

Hygiene was minimal. Heidnik had brought a
portajohn in for the women to use as a toilet, and for
feminine hygiene he brought them tampons. But in the
early days he refused to let them bathe. The only way
they had of cleaning themselves was with disposable
premoistened towels of the type many parents use on babies when changing their diapers. One day Thomas accidentally pulled two of the towels out of the container,
which sent Heidnik into a rage. Accusing her of wasting
property, he laid into her with the shovel handle.

Later he relented and every day would take one of
them upstairs to wash. They always carried their chains
with them, even into the bathtub. After they soaked for a
few minutes, Heidnik would push them into bed and
have sex with them.

While the cleanliness situation improved somewhat,
the food situation deteriorated.

One day he was feeding his two dogs, a huge part-Lab
he called Bear and a scruffy mutt of collie descent named

Flaky, and he had an idea. The next time one of the women needed to be punished, he grabbed a can of chicken-flavored dog food and ordered them all to eat. They balked. "Eat it or take a beating," he commanded. They ate it. From then on dog food became a regular part of their diet. Later it would take on a much more grisly aspect.

There were, however, occasions when he bent his rules. On Christmas Day he brought a takeout menu from a Chinese restaurant into the basement and let them pick their meal.

On January 18 their number grew by one more with the addition of Jacquelyn Askins, a petite, soft-spoken eighteen-year-old. Despite her childlike qualities, Askins was no naïf. At lunchtime that day she had been working the street in front of a seedy northside hotel, hoping somebody would come along looking for a nooner. That somebody turned out to be Heidnik, who was driving his blue Dodge van with the imitation fur interior, the one he fancifully referred to as "Bugs Bunny."

She went home with him and, according to the established pattern, was dragged into the cellar. As soon as they got downstairs, Heidnik grabbed a plastic rod and hit her five times across the buttocks.

"That's what you're going to get if you don't do what I tell you," he said.

To impress that upon her, he hit her five more times.

When he went to shackle her in the customary fashion, with muffler clamps, he discovered her ankles were so small she could slip right through the devices. So he had to use a pair of handcuffs.

That night he was in an merry mood. He not only had a new recruit, but he thought both Rivera and Lindsay were pregnant. It turned out to be a false alarm; none of the women, despite Heidnik's efforts, ever conceived. A

psychiatrist would later testify that Heidnik became extremely depressed when he saw the women at a court
hearing "and all their stomachs were flat." Dr. Clancy
McKenzie said Heidnik "took one look at them and told
himself, 'All that for nothing.'"

There was, however, in addition to his mistaken belief
in their pregnancies, another reason for celebrating: the
next day was Rivera's twenty-sixth birthday. In honor of
the double occasion he brought home more Chinese food
and a bottle of champagne, a luxury the women had
never expected to see. While they eagerly gulped it down,
Heidnik stood by and sipped slowly from a small glass.
Drinking was not one of his vices.

Chapter 15

October 1985–April 1986

A few weeks after Gary Heidnik's visit to the matrimonial bureau, a starry-eyed Filipina named Betty Disto was thumbing through a pen-pal brochure when a certain paragraph caught her eye. American male, it said. Single. Age: thirty-six. Occupation: nurse. She grabbed a piece of stationery and fired off a note of introduction to the person who placed the listing: Gary Heidnik, Philadelphia, PA.

A friendship-by-correspondence flowered. He sent her a color picture. It showed an intense-looking, dark-haired man with a thin but rather handsome face. She was unaccustomed to close contact with Caucasian males; she could not tell from the snapshot that he was actually five years older than he had claimed in the brochure. On the back of the picture there was a message: "Dearest Betty, Greetings from the land of ice and snow. Your friend, Gary."

She sent a picture of herself by return mail. Heidnik opened the envelope, stared at the image of a raven-haired young woman with dark eyes, a pouty mouth, and smooth, yellow skin. She said she was in her early twenties, but she looked younger. Absolutely ravishing. He smiled. Here was his Oriental beauty.

In a lengthy interview with Michael E. Ruane of the

Philadelphia Inquirer, before she went into virtual seclusion, Betty spoke fondly of those months of getting acquainted.

For almost two years, she said, they exchanged letters (Betty wrote every week) and, occasionally, telephone calls. In one transpacific hookup, Heidnik told her he was a minister in a church he had founded. It sounded strange to her, but people in America did strange things. Then he proposed.

This created something of a crisis in the Disto household, halfway across the world and a thousand years away. She was the youngest of six children. Her father, a former military man and rural policeman, had died when she was twelve. Her mother was not anxious for her to leave the nest, especially when it involved a trip to an unknown land among unknown people. "Don't go," her mother urged, arguing that Betty knew virtually nothing about the man. He might be a witch; a voodoo man. Betty laughed. Her mind was made up.

She applied for and received a visa. Heidnik sent her a ticket. Then she packed a suitcase, and on September 29, 1985, boarded a plane for a long, wearying trip: Manila to Tokyo to New York to Philadelphia.

Heidnik was waiting for her, wearing a favored black-leather vest, black trousers, and a black shirt. Later she would reflect on that first encounter. "He looked old," she told Ruane. Then shivering slightly, "He looked like Dracula."

That day, however, she was too excited to be very perceptive. He kissed her chastely on the cheek and welcomed her to the United States. This public display of affection embarrassed her. People didn't do that where she came from.

Since they were not yet married, she said, he wondered if she would be more comfortable at a hotel. "No," she replied. "Don't worry about it. I trust you."

Those were her days of innocence. They didn't last long.

When they got to North Marshall Street, Heidnik ushered her into a bedroom that contained a waterbed. She had never seen a waterbed and was a little uncomfortable at the thought of sleeping on one. She became even more uncomfortable when she discovered she was going to have to share it with a retarded black woman who was already snoring away. She had never seen a black person up close before either.

"Who is this?" she asked.

"A tenant," Heidnik replied. "She rents the room for two hundred fifty dollars a month. That isn't bad, is it?"

Betty didn't know what to say, so she didn't say anything.

It was a whirlwind romance. On October 3, before she even had a chance to recover from her jet lag, Betty drove with Heidnik to Elkton, Maryland, where they were married. Afterwards they returned to Philadelphia and checked into the Marriott. Then they went back to North Marshall Street.

For a while he treated her as though she were a princess, calling her "honey" and doing whatever he could to please her. They talked about having children, and Heidnik said he really wanted a son. If she had a boy, he said, he wanted to name him Jesse after King David's father in the Old Testament.

The honeymoon lasted a week.

One day she came home from shopping and heard a strange noise in the bedroom. Nudging open the door, she peeked inside and had the shock of her life. Her husband was in bed with three black women. All of them were naked and twisted into strange positions. She cried out, turned and ran down the stairs, sobbing hysterically.

Heidnik ran after her. "Give me a ticket," she said. "I'll go home."

"No," Heidnik said. "You don't understand. That is normal here in America."

"I can't stand it," she sobbed.

"You're going to have to," Heidnik said. "I'm the boss."

From then on it got worse.

Heidnik spent a lot of time hanging out near the Elwyn Institute. On Sundays he held "services" at the North Marshall Street house, jamming the place with a couple of dozen handicapped people—the world's outcasts, who had either physical or mental deformities and were ashamed to go to regular church because people stared at them.

Betty estimates she attended twenty of these "services," and never saw Heidnik accept a penny. It was against the church "constitution" to pass a collection plate. In addition, if any of them were having a hard time or were temporarily homeless, Heidnik would let them stay there with him and Betty.

This did not mean he had given up other women. He would bring home retarded clients from Elwyn or hookers he picked up on the street. Never during the entire time she was there, Betty said, was there not another woman in the house.

When she complained, he would give her a withering look with eyes that changed in a flash from calm and cool to flashing and murderous. Then he'd punch her, usually on the arms, and punish her. He'd make her stand in the corner for up to twelve hours at a time. He would refuse her food. Or he'd laugh and make her watch him have sex, then force her to cook for him and his partner or partners.

Sunday, January 12, 1986, was a particularly bad day; a day when Heidnik was even more violent than usual. When she complained yet again about his lifestyle, he grabbed her by the hair, slapped her face, and punched her on the arms and legs. Then he forced her to submit to regular and rectal intercourse.

"If you run away, I'll kill you," he told her.

A stranger in a strange land, she didn't know where to turn. Finally, in desperation, she made contact with other members of the Filipino community. They urged her to leave.

Four days later, three and a half months after she arrived, she put her passport and a spare dress in a plastic bag and hid it outside. Saying she was going shopping, she slipped out the door, picked up her bundle and fled. She also reported him to the cops.

On January 27 the district attorney's office charged Heidnik with spousal rape, involuntary deviate sexual intercourse, simple assault, and indecent assault. He was picked up two days later, the precise day his parole expired on the Alberta Davidson incident.

In March Betty failed to appear at a preliminary hearing called to determine if there was enough evidence to hold him for trial. Without her testimony there was no case, so the judge had no choice but to dismiss the charges.

Heidnik didn't know it, but Betty was pregnant. On September 15 she delivered Heidnik's child, a boy she named Jesse John, nicknamed J.J. She sent him a postcard telling him about it.

Over the months she steadfastly refused to divorce him. At the time of his trial they were still officially married, but she virtually boycotted the proceedings. But then again, so did Heidnik's father and brother.

Chapter 16

January 14, 1987

Separated or not, Betty Heidnik expected financial support. When her husband fell dreadfully behind in his $135 a week payments, which didn't even factor in J.J., she hauled him into court. She did not know it, but Gary Heidnik had more pressing things on his mind.

Thirteen days after he added Deborah Dudley to his basement group—four days before he would pick up Jacquelyn Askins—he appeared before Judge Stephen E. Levin Jr. in the family court division of Common Pleas Court. If it were not such a serious issue, it would be humorous. A transcript of the proceeding has overtones of a Smothers Brothers skit. What makes it particularly interesting, though, is it is one of the few public recordings of a dialogue with Gary Heidnik. Although he took the stand during his 1978 trial, that was a set performance. With Levin, however, there was give and take. Heidnik, acting as his own lawyer, jousted with the judge. Actually played games with him. The judge didn't appreciate it. He came very close to throwing Heidnik in jail for contempt. If he had, the saga of the women in the cellar might have had a very different ending.

At the time, Heidnik probably was feeling pretty cocky. He had four women in the basement, two of whom he thought were pregnant. He thought his plan was working. And then along came Judge Levin and his runaway wife to try to screw things up.

Judge Levin opened the proceedings by reminding Heidnik of a decision the previous August ordering him to pay support to Betty. J.J. had not then been born.

"There are allegations in the file," Judge Levin began, "that defendant [Heidnik] has substantial assets, and, number one, the plaintiff [Betty] would like an increased amount on the arrearages, and, secondly, I believe there is a problem in having the wages attached. The record indicated that the VA will not deduct the ordered child support amount from the check. Is that so, sir?"

"I'm," Heidnik stuttered, "I'm still having a problem where you said I had a lot of assets."

Judge Levin: "Well, according to the court record, you have twenty-eight thousand—"

Heidnik: "If I got that, I sure would like to know where it's at."

"Well, either we have a mistake here or we have the wrong case. Do you have an account with Merrill Lynch?"

"No."

"Do you have a bank account?"

"Yes, sir."

"How much is in your bank account?"

"About two thousand."

"Okay," said Levin.

"I'd like to know where the rest of that's at," Heidnik added.

For the next several minutes they skirmished. Levin probed. Heidnik played coy. Judge Levin was able to get Heidnik to admit he received about $400 a month in Social Security.

"Okay. Let me ask you a question," said Levin. "Why are you getting Social Security and disability? What is the problem?"

"You mean what's my medical problem?"

"You must have a problem. Social Security does not give money to a healthy man . . . at your age. So something is the problem."

"Yeah. I . . . I got a nervous disorder."

"All right," Judge Levin responded. "Now how much do you receive from the VA a month?"

Heidnik reluctantly admitted it was about $1,300.

After a long discussion about Heidnik's alleged inability to remove his common-law wife (Dorothy, circa 1971) from his Social Security records, the topic swung back to Heidnik's VA checks.

"How long have you been on disability?" Judge Levin asked.

"About twenty, twenty-one years."

"Oh. Okay. In other words—"

"Well, in actuality, since I got out of the service."

"When did you get out of the service?"

"I got out of the service . . . I got out in '63."

"Okay."

"And then—"

"So when you got out of the service, at one point, you claimed—"

"Then, in '66, they made me a hundred percent. I was, like, ten percent or something in between there."

The discussion took another abrupt turn. Back to Social Security. Heidnik claimed one reason he was behind in his support was because he had been unable to convince the Social Security office to replace Dorothy with Betty on his monthly checks.

Judge Levin prompted: "Then, when you came with Betty, they said, 'How can you prove she's your wife? You still have the other wife.' "

"Yeah," Heidnik agreed. "Something like that."

"Okay. Now I understand."

"But then I tried to tell them I hadn't seen the woman [Dorothy]. They had actually taken her off. My understanding was that they had taken her off my checks. See,

I was getting money for both me and her. Not Betty, but the other woman, right? And then something like '78, '79, '80, somewhere around there, they actually took that woman off my checks and I was only getting money for me. So I . . . I assumed that they had dissolved the marriage, the VA, because, you know, that was the only place, you know, it was registered, so to speak. Then, when I went in to get Betty on the checks, they dropped that one on me."

Judge Levin decided to explore Heidnik's mental history.

"What is your mental problem, sir?"

"What is my mental problem?"

"Yes."

"You know, the doctors aren't too specific about that when they talk to me about that. They . . . they have me going to group therapy every month and I . . . I get medicine. Things like that."

"Mr. Heidnik," Levin said, getting back to money, "didn't you have eleven thousand dollars in Fidelity in 1986?"

"That's possible."

"What happened to that money?"

"Well, I bought Betty a car, for one thing."

"When did you buy her a car?"

" 'Eighty-six."

" 'Eighty-five, sir," interjected Betty Heidnik.

"Oh. 'Eighty-five?" Heidnik queried.

"You had $11,902 in a bank account in 1986," Levin pressed. "What happened to that money?"

"I'm . . . I'm paying a mortgage on a house, for one thing."

"You still have it there, don't you?" Levin asked accusingly.

"No, I don't. You're talking about Fidelity?"

"Yes . . . What happened to the Fidelity money?"

"It's down to about two thousand now."

"It is down two thousand? There is only nine thousand there?"

"No. No. It's down to about two thousand."

"What happened to the nine thousand?"

"I spent it."

Seeing he was getting nowhere, Judge Levin switched to the church.

"What is the United Church of the Ministers of God?" he asked Heidnik.

"That's the church I belong to."

"Are you the bishop?"

"It's an honorary title."

"Whose money is at Merrill Lynch?"

"Merrill Lynch?"

"Yes."

"Merrill Lynch's, I guess."

This must have angered Levin. "You do not have any money at Merrill Lynch?" he asked.

"No, I do not."

"Well, do you control money for the United Church of the Ministers of God? Do you personally handle their money?"

"Yeah. I guess you could say that."

"Well, how much money do you handle for them?"

"I just cost them about eighty thousand. So it went down a little bit."

"You cost them eighty thousand?" Judge Levin asked in disbelief.

"See, there was a stock called Crazy Eddie's—"

"Yes."

"—and I bought it around sixteen, and it's down around nine now. I'm not too popular after that little move. I couldn't resist Crazy Eddie, though."

"Well, how did you buy it? Who gave you the authority to buy it?"

"The board of directors."

"Who is the board of directors?"

"Reverend Mosley. My brother. What the heck's her last name?"

"You are saying the money in Merrill Lynch is not your money?"

"No. It's the church's money."

"It is the church's money. Why did you not tell me about it? Why are you being evasive?"

"You asked me if I have any money—"

"Sir, you are being evasive."

"No. You asked me—"

"Do you know what the word evasive means?"

"Yeah, I think so."

"I think you do too. You are jerking my chain. You know all about the Merrill Lynch account. You had three hundred thousand dollars in the Merrill Lynch account. Over three hundred thousand dollars."

"That's not my money."

"Then why didn't you tell me, 'It wasn't my money'?"

"I did. You said did I have any money with Merrill Lynch. I said no, I do not. You're talking about my money, right? I do not have any money with Merrill Lynch."

"It is their money?"

"The church's money."

"How about the Fidelity bank account?"

"That's my money."

"And how much is in the bank account right now?"

"Two thousand, roughly."

"And what happened to the other nine?"

"Well, I . . . I didn't itemize it, but I know, like, I paid my gas bill, which they were going to shut off. I put a thousand dollars in my car, which was falling apart, at Pep Boys over there. I've got receipts for that one, like I said."

Judge Levin was weary. "Okay," he said.

After discussing the possibility of getting money for J.J. with Betty, he promised not to let the matter drop.

"We are going to have another hearing as soon as I have a mental health evaluation on him," he dictated for the record. "I am going to ask our department to look at him and ask for his VA records, so that I can know who I am dealing with. I do not know who I am dealing with. I am looking at a man who appears to be very intelligent, who appears to be evasive. I do not know whether that is deliberate or he really is answering honestly. I cannot tell, all right? I know that he had control of over three hundred thousand dollars. I do not know whether that is his money or the church money."

Turning to Heidnik, Judge Levin offered one piece of advice: "Hold on to the Crazy Eddie stock. It may go up."

The tests Judge Levin ordered were performed in March. By that time things were going very badly for Heidnik. In January he was haughty; in March his personality almost certainly was entirely different. When he took the tests, two of his captives had died. It was a time of extreme crisis. The tests were very revealing. But they came too late.

Chapter 17

February 7, 1987

Sandra Lindsay looked like hell. For a week she had been dangling by her wrist from an overhead beam in a punishment session that began because she tried to push aside the plywood sheet covering "the hole." The punishment dragged on when she refused to eat and Heidnik, still believing her to be pregnant, tried to force-feed her. He shoved small pieces of bread in her mouth and then held his hand over her lips until she swallowed.

But she was wearing down. For the last couple of days she had been vomiting and she complained of a fever. Heidnik ignored her and kept insisting that she eat.

Josefina Rivera knew a crisis was coming when she looked up and saw that Lindsay had slumped down and showed no signs of rising. Realizing it would just make Heidnik angrier if he came down and found her like that, Rivera and the other three began yelling encouragement to the semiconscious woman. She didn't move.

About that time Heidnik came down the stairs, took one look at Lindsay and ordered her to stand up. She did and he left. However, a few minutes later she collapsed again. This time when Heidnik came down, he did more than talk to her.

He unconnected her handcuffs and she dropped to the

floor in a heap. Heidnik angrily kicked her into the hole. "She's faking," he said.

Turning his back on her, he walked over to a large chest-type freezer on the other side of the room and dished out three bowls of ice cream. He handed one to Rivera, one to Thomas, and kept one for himself. He took his upstairs. When he came back a few minutes later and saw that Lindsay still had not moved, he dragged her out of the hole and tried to find a pulse. There wasn't one. She was dead.

Heidnik looked at her for a minute and then said, "She choked on a piece of bread."

Her death presented a major problem for him. It not only set back his plan to gather a group of human baby machines, but also he had to figure out what to do with the body. If he put it somewhere and it were found, she could be identified. And if she were identified, she could be traced to him. Now and then, her sister or cousins still came by looking for her. He simply couldn't get rid of the body, he reasoned; he had to destroy it.

Hoisting Lindsay over his shoulder like a sack of cement, Heidnik carried her up the steps. Sometime later the women in the basement heard what they thought was a power saw. They looked at each other and shivered.

Heidnik's dogs, Flaky and Bear, had the run of the house. Occasionally, when the door to upstairs was open, they would bring some of their food into the basement and take it under the pool table across the room to eat. Several hours after Heidnik disappeared with Lindsay's body, Bear came down dragging a long white bone with chunks of red meat clinging to it. The women looked at the bone, then they looked at each other, and each thought the same thing: I wish I were close enough to grab the meat.

Investigators later were unable to find bloodstains on an electric saw found in Heidnik's house, prompting them to believe he got rid of the tool used to carve up Lindsay. A few days after Lindsay died, he bought a food processor, and while no bloodstains or body parts were found on it, investigators are convinced he used it to grind up parts of Lindsay's body. He mixed the processed meat with dog food and fed it, he told Rivera, to Flaky, Bear, and the surviving captives. What he did not immediately grind he put in white plastic bags, which he stacked neatly in the freezer compartment of his upstairs refrigerator.

The parts he could not grind—the head, hands, feet, and rib cage—he tried to destroy by cooking. That created a terrible stench, though, which almost choked the women in the basement and was so pervasive it had the entire neighborhood up in arms.

Although the neighbors yelled for the police, a rookie cop answered the call and went away when Heidnik told him he had simply overcooked the roast he was preparing for dinner. The smell hung around for days: polluting the air; permeating what little clothing they had; and, most noticeably, virtually soaking into Heidnik himself. That night, for the first time since he took his first captive on November 26, Heidnik did not come down to the basement demanding sex. But for many days afterwards, when he resumed his sex-fix visits, he smelled so strongly of burning flesh it was all the women could do to keep from gagging.

Heidnik didn't know it yet, but his days were numbered; his grandiose plans for creating a basement baby factory were rapidly unraveling. Before they collapsed completely, however, his captives would undergo a lot more suffering and one more of them would die.

Chapter 18

After Sandra Lindsay's death, Heidnik became even more paranoid. Convinced now that the women were plotting against him, he encouraged an informer system so he could stop any escape plans before they got started. The reward for snitching would be exemption from the hole, a little better food, and slightly more freedom.

Heidnik's paranoia about escape plans was not totally unjustified. At one time the four women worked out a scheme whereby Deborah Dudley was going to hit Heidnik over the head with a piece of iron pipe they had dug up and the others would grab whatever was handy and stab him. Askins later testified at Heidnik's trial that before they could put the plan into effect, Rivera tipped him off.

Heidnik also had decided that he could keep them even more off balance if they didn't know where he was, whether he was upstairs or out of the house altogether. When he was home they could easily hear him walking, and when he left they could hear the door close and his car drive away. The way to solve that, he figured, was to stop them from hearing him. That led to one of the most cruel tortures he was ever to use against the women.

One by one he took Deborah Dudley, Lisa Thomas, and Jacquelyn Askins over to the eye hook and cuffed them with one hand above their heads. He also cuffed their feet. Then he stuffed a plastic bag in their mouths as a gag and secured it with duct tape wound around their heads. Finally, looping an arm around their throats to hold them still, he took a screwdriver and gouged in their ears, trying to damage the eardrums.

"He used three kinds of screwdrivers," Thomas swore later, "small, medium, and large. He twisted them in our ears until pus came out."

Again, Rivera was exempt.

Heidnik's chief antagonist during this period was Deborah Dudley, who fought him in everything he tried to do. One day, in an attempt to frighten her into submission, he unhooked her and dragged her upstairs. They were gone only a few minutes, and when they returned, Dudley was uncharacteristically quiet. Rivera was particularly inquisitive. "What happened?" she asked. "What did he do?"

Finally Dudley whispered, "He showed me Sandra Lindsay's head in a pot. And he had her ribs in a roasting pan and a bunch of her other body parts in the freezer. He told me if I didn't start listening to him, that was going to happen to me too."

The sight didn't chastise her for long; within a day or two she was again pushing him as far as she could.

About this time Heidnik introduced still another new torture: electric shock.

Heidnik snipped off the plug end of an ordinary electrical extension cord and stripped the insulation to leave a bare wire. Then he plugged the other end into a socket. With current then flowing through the wire, he touched the bare end to the women's chains and laughed while they jumped and screamed. For extra effect he submerged them in water.

On Wednesday, March 18, he decided all the women

except Rivera needed punishment, so he put them in the hole and stood by while Rivera filled the pit with water using a hose and a nearby faucet. Earlier he had drilled several holes in the plywood covering as air vents. When the women were in the hole they could see a little of what was going on in the basement.

On this day they crouched in the hole in fear. They knew what was coming. Thomas, physically the largest of the three, was on the floor of the pit with Askins and Dudley in her lap. Through one of the air holes they could see the wire. They watched as it inched toward their chains, which snaked out of the hole around a pipe. When the bare wire touched a metal link, the current shot through their bodies. They screamed.

"I couldn't see Nicole with the wire, but I could hear her saying she had it," Thomas said later.

The wire went straight to Dudley's chain, so she took the heaviest jolt. "He's killing me," she shrieked.

She was right. Seconds later she went limp. Thomas and Askins heard a splash and looked over. Dudley was bent over, face down in the muddy pool.

"She's dead," Thomas yelled. "You've killed her. I don't feel no pulse."

Heidnik, thinking the wire was faulty, had run upstairs to get another one. When he returned Rivera told him that Thomas claimed Debbie was dead.

"No," Heidnik replied, "nothing's wrong with Debbie. I don't want to hear that bullshit."

Thomas lifted the board. "Something's wrong with Debbie," she said. "She's dead."

Heidnik walked over to the pit and looked in. "You know, Debbie's face is down in the water," he told Rivera.

"Hold your hand up," he told Thomas, unfastening the cuff that linked her to Dudley. He lifted Askins out of the hole and then reached for Thomas, but she looked to be in shock. He grabbed her arm, lifted her out, and pulled her clear. Then he bent down and pulled Dudley's body out.

The next thing Thomas knew she was stretched out on the concrete basement floor and her handcuffs had been removed. She looked up and saw Heidnik calmly making dog food sandwiches. A few feet away was Dudley's body.

"Aren't you glad it wasn't one of you," Heidnik commented conversationally. Nodding at the dead Dudley, he added, "That's the asshole that caused Sandy's death."

After making them sandwiches, Heidnik went upstairs, returning a few minutes later carrying writing implements. Handing a clean sheet of paper and a pen to Rivera, he told her to write.

"Put the date at the top," he said. "March eighteenth, 1987." She did.

"Now the time."

She scribbled in "6:30 P.M."

"Now write this: 'I, Nicole Rivera, and Gary Heidnik killed Debbie Johnson (Dudley) by applying electricity to her chain while sitting in a pool of water in a hole in a basement of 3520 Marshall Street.' "

He ordered her to sign it, then added his signature below hers. He also commanded Askins and Thomas to sign it as witnesses.

"Now I've got the letter," he told Rivera. "If you ever go to the cops, I can use this as evidence that you killed Debbie."

Bending over, he unlocked Rivera's shackles and told her to go upstairs and put on a clean shirt and a pair of pants. It was the first time in almost four months that she had not been chained. It also was the first time she had worn a pair of pants. The others enviously watched her go.

* * *

Heidnik left Dudley's body on the floor overnight. The next morning he wrapped her head and feet in plastic and carried the body over to the freezer. After shuffling some of his cartons of ice cream and other foodstuffs, he laid the body inside, closed the lid, and put several bags of dirt on top. Then he started making plans to dispose of it. Since no one could connect him to Dudley as they could have to Sandra Lindsay, he was not faced with the same constraints. This body he would simply dump as soon as he found a suitable spot. With her safely in the freezer, though, there was no hurry. He went upstairs to find Rivera. That night he would give her a treat. They would go out to eat.

Chapter 19

March 18–March 23, 1987

Following Deborah Dudley's death, Josefina Rivera's life-style improved considerably.

Secure in the belief that the letter he had Rivera sign protected him from treachery, Heidnik treated her more as a girlfriend and less as a captive. One night they went to the McDonald's near the Elwyn Institute where Heidnik used to hang out. Heidnik chose it specifically so his friends could see him with another woman and rein-force his contention that Sandra Lindsay was not with him. While there, they ran into Tony Brown and Gail. They asked if he knew where Sandy was.

"I think her family has her stashed away somewhere so they can cash her Social Security checks," Heidnik re-plied.

After that they went to a home-supply store so Heidnik could get two new cabinets for his kitchen.

One day they went to an auto-supply store, where Heidnik purchased a can of transmission fluid for his Rolls. They took the Rolls to a garage for repairs.

They did the fast-food circuit, all the places Heidnik liked to go: McDonald's, Roy Rogers, Denny's, Wendy's. At one restaurant Rivera and Heidnik held hands.

They went shopping for a new wig for Rivera. They had sex. He took her into his confidence.

"If I ever get caught," he told her, "I'm going to act crazy. I'm going to go into court and salute everybody." He bragged that he could beat the tests. "I know them inside and out," he said. "I've learned so I can keep getting my government checks."

One night they drove across the Delaware River into New Jersey. When they got to a forested area known as the Pine Barrens, Heidnik stopped, flicked on his brights and looked around. "This place would be perfect to dump Debbie's body," he told Rivera.

On the way back they stopped at a flea market and a record shop so Heidnik could buy an album and four or five 45s.

Just before midnight on Saturday, March 22, Heidnik said it was time to take care of Dudley. "Get a blanket," he ordered, "and spread it on the kitchen floor."

He went into the cellar, got Dudley's body out of the freezer, and carried it upstairs, stretching it out on the blanket.

"I want you to look at her," he told Rivera.

"I don't want to," she said.

He insisted, peeling back the plastic from her face. "Look," he commanded. "It will make you strong."

Rivera took a quick peek.

Heidnik carried the body into the backyard and loaded it into the trunk of his old Dodge Dart, which would not be nearly as conspicuous as his Cadillac. They returned to the Pine Barrens and drove down a dirt road. After a few minutes Heidnik stopped. No lights were visible for miles.

"This looks good enough," he said.

Rivera huddled in the car while Heidnik retrieved Dudley's body from the trunk and carried it across an open space to a grove of trees. She could hear the twigs crunching as he walked.

In a few minutes he was back. Throwing his black leather gloves on the dash, he sped away. When they got back to Philadelphia he stopped to buy a newspaper. "I want to check my stocks," he told Rivera.

The next day he brought up the subject of finding a replacement for Dudley. His harem was now down to two—Thomas and Askins—if you didn't count Rivera. He was a long way from the ten-woman group he envisioned as ideal.

On Monday night, March 23, he and Rivera piled into his Cadillac and drove around looking for a candidate. It didn't take them long before they saw a face they both recognized.

Standing on a corner, waiting for a customer, was a small, dark, twenty-four-year-old woman named Agnes Adams. Rivera knew her as "Vickie" and she knew Rivera as "Nicole." They knew each other from a strip club called Hearts and Flowers where they both had worked in the past.

Heidnik also knew her, but not by name. He had picked her up one night in January, apparently looking for some sex outside his basement crowd. At that time he had agreed to pay her thirty-five dollars for oral sex and she had climbed into his Cadillac and driven with him to North Marshall Street. When they got there, a car was parked across the entrance to Heidnik's driveway and he was unable to find a parking place anywhere in the vicinity. He paid her ten dollars for her time and took her back downtown.

She had seen him again in February, when he picked her up at noon from the corner of Fifth and Girard. This time he had better luck getting into his driveway. He took her into the kitchen, gave her a soda, and watched while she played a couple of games on Mr. Do. Then they went upstairs and she performed fellatio on him. He paid her thirty-five dollars, saw her out the door, and locked it behind her. She walked home. He made no attempt to capture her and make her part of his cellar group. He was picky about whom he selected.

This time, however, the situation was different.

He negotiated a thirty-dollar price with her, and the three of them—Heidnik, Rivera, and Adams—drove to North Marshall Street. When they got there, Heidnik gave Rivera the key and told her to lock up. He and Adams went upstairs and had sex, followed by what some cynics now refer to as the "Heidnik maneuver." He choked her, cuffed her, took her downstairs and threw her in the hole. Rivera remained in the kitchen, sipping wine coolers.

"That was easy," Heidnik said to Rivera. "We can do that again tomorrow."

Rivera just nodded. She had plans of her own.

Chapter 20

March 24-25, 1987

Josefina Rivera sensed it was time for her to make her move. All day Tuesday, March 24, she worked on Heidnik, convincing him she needed to see her family. After all, she had been gone for four months. If he let her do that, she said, she promised to find another woman for him.

Heidnik finally agreed. He had the letter, didn't he? "But if you try to run," he cautioned, "I'll kill the others."

Late that night they left in Heidnik's Cadillac. Everything was quiet in the cellar. The new arrival, Adams, was in the hole, and Thomas and Askins were curled up on the mattress. After Dudley's death, Heidnik had eased up considerably and provided the cellar dwellers with pillows, blankets, and even a TV.

According to the plan, Heidnik would drop Rivera, who would go see her children, pick up a woman she knew, and meet him back at a gas station parking lot at Sixth and Girard at about midnight.

As soon as Heidnik drove off, Rivera beelined to the apartment of her boyfriend, Vincent Nelson, four blocks away.

Nelson was shocked. This woman had walked out on him in the middle of an argument four months ago and he hadn't heard a word from her since. Now here she was, he told police later, banging on his door and ringing his door bell at the same time and ranting about somebody who had been holding her captive.

"She came in, and as we were walking up the steps, she was rambling on, you know, talking real fast about this guy having three girls chained up in the basement of this house and she was held hostage for four months. She said that two of the girls were dead and he had three more in a hole in the basement floor chained up and he was going to kill them if she doesn't come back with another girl in a certain amount of time."

The more she talked, the less believable her story became.

"She said that he was beating them, raping them, had them eating dead people, just like he was a cold-blooded nut. Dogs was in the yard eating people bones. I just thought she was crazy. I really didn't believe it, and I still don't believe this shit.

"I said I was going up there with a hammer and I was going to fuck him up, and she said, 'No, that might scare him and he might go back and kill the girls.' "

According to what Nelson later told *Inquirer* reporter A. Paolantonio, he and Rivera left his apartment and started walking toward Sixth and Girard. However, when they got about a block away, Nelson reconsidered and decided it would be better to call the cops.

They stopped at a pay phone. Nelson dialed 911 and handed the receiver to Rivera. At first the cops didn't believe her either. An officer told her to stay where she was and a unit would be there presently.

Minutes later officers David Savidge and John Cannon pulled up.

As everyone else had been that night, Savidge and Cannon were skeptical. The story Rivera disgorged was just too wild to be true. Then they looked at the abrasions and scars on her ankles where she said the chains had been, and they became believers.

After Rivera told them Heidnik was waiting for her three blocks away, Savidge and Cannon wasted no time getting there. They coasted into the lot and pulled up behind a 1987 pewter-over-white Cadillac. The vehicle's engine was running, and there was a man sitting behind the wheel.

Cannon, a short, compact man with graying hair, took the passenger side; Savidge, a heavily-built blond a head taller than his partner, approached on the driver's side. They had their weapons drawn. Heidnik saw Savidge coming and he raised his hands.

"What's this all about, officer?" he asked in surprise. "Didn't I make my child support?"

Savidge studied him closely. "No," he replied quietly, "it's a little more serious than that."

He cuffed Heidnik and took him to the Sex Crimes Unit building where Rivera was being questioned in more detail.

Again, Heidnik looked at Savidge.

"Is it child support?" he repeated.

Savidge thought he sounded like a broken record.

"No," Savidge told him for the second time. "It's about kidnapping, rape, and homicide."

Still, it was a song Heidnik would sing all night: that the police really wanted him for missing his child-support payments.

Chapter 21

March 25, 1987
4:30 A.M.

Sergeant Frank McCloskey was ready for some action. He had been on call outside 3520 North Marshall Street for the last four and a half hours, waiting for a command to do something. When he first got to the scene, he did the same thing Officer Julio Aponte had done forty-three days earlier. He knocked on the doors. He tried the handles. He checked out the windows. He got nowhere. When he called in to report his lack of success, the dispatcher told him to sit tight.

All he knew was that a man named Gary Heidnik had been arrested about midnight after a near-hysterical woman called the Twenty-fifth District and spun some wild tale about how she had been a captive in this house for four months and three women were believed to be alive and still in the cellar. He had to wait until they got a search warrant before he could go busting in.

Just before five, more police showed up. They had the warrant. Among the new arrivals was Officer David Savidge, who had been the first to hear Rivera's story face to face.

While Savidge and McCloskey watched, another sergeant tried unsuccessfully to open the doors with keys he had gotten from Heidnik. When he saw the keys weren't going to work, Homicide Lieutenant James Hansen called for a crowbar.

Next door, Doris Zibulka was sleeping. When Hansen went to work with the crowbar, she thought *she* was being raided. "They just about knocked me out of bed."

Once the door was down, Hansen dashed for the kitchen; Savidge and McCloskey headed for the basement.

All around the room, McCloskey noted, were white plastic shopping bags. A mattress was lying in the middle of the room and on it were two black women, covered in blankets and snuggled up against each other for warmth. They were asleep.

When they heard the commotion, they jerked awake and started screaming.

"Police," McCloskey yelled. "We're the police. We're here to help you. No one is going to hurt you."

The women bolted to their feet, letting the blanket drop. Except for socks, they were both nude from the waist down. Both had shackles on their ankles and were connected to heavy chains. One was Lisa Thomas, the other was Jacquelyn Askins.

"Are there any other women in the house?" McCloskey asked. "Is anyone here but you?"

Both pointed to a pile of white plastic bags sitting on a board on the other side of the room.

"She's there," Thomas said.

McCloskey, remembering the woman's tale included a story about dismemberment, picked up one of the plastic bags.

"Here?" he asked incredulously.

"No, under the board," Thomas replied. "She's in the hole."

McCloskey pushed away the bags and slid the board aside. Squatting at the bottom of the shallow pit was Agnes Adams. She tried to stand up, lost her balance and tottered. McCloskey grabbed her arm and lifted her out.

She was completely nude. She was shackled like the others, and in addition, her hands were cuffed behind her back.

She started screaming too.

"It's all right," McCloskey said. "We're here to help you."

"We're free!" Thomas and Askins yelled. "It's the police!" They grabbed McCloskey's hands and smothered them with kisses. "We're saved!" they shrieked.

Adams was still in shock. "He took my thirty dollars," she yelled angrily. "Get my thirty dollars back."

"Don't worry about it," McCloskey said.

He dug out his handcuff key and tried to unlock the bracelets binding Adams' hands. It didn't fit.

"Try this one," another officer said, proffering his cuff key. It did the trick. They then worked at removing the leg irons.

McCloskey noted that their ankles were covered with bruises and sores. Some were fresh and some had been scabbed over. They couldn't undo the nuts, and sent word upstairs to fetch some bolt cutters. They also called for an ambulance and some extra hospital shifts for the women to wear.

They were so skinny, they looked like POWs. They said they were starving.

"Gary kept ice cream in the freezer," Askins said, pointing to the box where Deborah Dudley's body had been kept on hold until Heidnik had found a place to dump it. "Can we eat that?"

"I don't think you ought to have any ice cream yet," said McCloskey. "Wait until the doctors check you over."

When their ankles had been freed and they were taken to the ambulance, they went through the dining room where Heidnik had left some cookies on the table. They grabbed them and wolfed them down.

With the women on their way to medical care, the

officers fanned out through the house. On the shelf in a closet they found a large stack of porno magazines, all of them featuring black women.

While McCloskey headed upstairs, Savidge went into the kitchen. He looked at the stove and noted an aluminum pot. The inside was scorched and covered with a yellowish material. In the open oven he saw a metal roasting pan that was charred on the inside and contained a piece of bone that looked suspiciously like a rib. On the counter was a heavy-duty food processor, obviously used. He opened the freezer and, right there on the front shelf, was a human forearm.

That was too much for even the veteran Savidge. Feeling the bile rise in his throat, he ran outside and gulped the fresh air, trying mightily to keep from vomiting.

Chapter 22

March 26, 1987

When the story broke, the news media went wild. There were so many lurid details to cover, reporters weren't sure which way to turn first. The crimes in themselves were gruesome enough: murder, rape, bondage, torture, dismemberment, and cannibalism. Race was involved. Plus, swirling in the background were twin specters guaranteed to get attention anytime they were tied to scandal: money and religion. Gary Heidnik definitely was not a penniless ghetto dweller, not with a stock portfolio at Merrill Lynch valued at some $550,000, even with the Crazy Eddie loss. The stock account was in the name of the United Church of the Ministers of God, but Heidnik also had a personal account, police later discovered, containing more than $16,000. There may be other accounts that police still haven't found.

It was a case of overload for the media; there were simply too many sensational elements for any newspaper to handle at once. But they tried.

The timing of Heidnik's arrest gave the newspaper break to Philadelphia's tabloid *Daily News*. When the paper's morning edition hit the street about eight A.M., there was a relatively small piece on page three headlined, YOUNG WOMEN FOUND CHAINED; HUMAN ARM DISCOVERED IN NORTH PHILADELPHIA REFRIGERATOR.

By the time the afternoon edition rolled off the press, though, Heidnik *was* the front page. HORROR ON MAR-SHALL STREET was the memo line, and in smaller type, *He put chains on my legs; victims tell of beatings, sex, and deaths of 2 women.* Inside were a half-dozen stories, including a profile on Heidnik compiled from interviews with neighbors. The main story was bannered, THREE CHAINED WOMEN FREED, HUMAN BODY PARTS FOUND; MAN ARRESTED.

The more staid *Inquirer* couldn't publish the information until the next day, but it compensated in length for what it lacked in immediacy. A bold, black banner across the entire eight columns of page one screamed, MAN HELD IN TORTURE KILLING, with *3 found chained in cellar* in smaller type. The story ran about halfway down the front page and took up most of an inside page. The paper also carried several ancillary stories.

When it was discovered that Heidnik was a self-proclaimed bishop in a church he created, and drove expensive cars, the headline writers went into passing gear.

On March 26 the *New York Post*'s main story was headlined, MADMAN'S SEX ORGY WITH CHAINED WOMEN, with the subhead, *Body parts found in Philly's house of horror.* A subordinate story dubbed Heidnik the "Rolls-Royce 'Reverend' " and proclaimed he was "into stocks & bondage."

Another New York tabloid, the *Daily News,* yelled, *Sex slaves & mutilation in Philadelphia,* and in larger type, FIND WOMEN CHAINED IN HORROR DUNGEON.

That same day *USA Today* said, PHILA. ROW HOUSE SITE OF DEATH, TERROR . . . *3 women chained; body parts are found.*

Even the ultraconservative *New York Times* got into it, albeit a bit more slowly. On March 27, a day behind most of the others, the *Times* devoted a quarter of a page to a story headlined, PROSECUTOR TO ASK DEATH PENALTY IN TORTURE CASE. Included in the spread were pictures of Heidnik, Tony Brown, and the North Marshall Street house.

The *Times* followed with a second story the next day, captioned, STRANGE PORTRAIT OF TORTURE SUSPECT.

Uncounted stories also were broadcast on radio and television. The facts were sent worldwide by the wire services. The man who would later be Heidnik's lawyer received a clipping from a friend in Australia.

Coverage in Philadelphia, of course, was voluminous, with the *Daily News* and the *Inquirer,* both owned by Knight-Ridder, devoting a task force of reporters and thousands of inches of print to the incident.

The intensity and breadth of the media coverage would prove to be an issue when it came time to select a jury to try the case. Heidnik's lawyer had no trouble digging up plenty of evidence to show that the *whole world* knew about his client's crimes.

Chapter 23

When police arrested Heidnik and freed Thomas, Askins, and Adams, their work was just beginning. It would take them days just to sift through the piles of paper and mounds of physical evidence they would need to present a comprehensive report. Whatever crimes Heidnik would be charged with, investigators fervently wished disorderly record keeping and slovenliness could be added to the list. Just the inventory of what he had on him when he was brought in by Savidge and Cannon was enough to cause immediate confusion.

In his pockets, among other things, was $1,962 in one-, five-, ten-, twenty-, fifty-, and hundred-dollar bills, along with a silver dollar and a half dollar. He had a bank card, a Sears credit card, a telephone card, a VA identification card, a driver's license, an ID card from his church carrying his picture in a clerical collar, and a nurse's identification card from the VA hospital at Coatesville. He had a pocket calculator, a gold Cross pen, a penknife, and a handcuff key. He had papers referring to a '72 Dodge, a '64 Plymouth, a '71 Cadillac, and a '73 Serro Scotty house trailer, some of which were in the name of his church and some of which were in his name. He had a stack of receipts from traffic court and a notice saying his driver's license had been suspended. He also had receipts from several retail stores and a statement from Merrill Lynch showing his account balance as of the previous October 31 was $577,382.52.

But that was as nothing compared to the list police made of items found in his house. It took them eleven days to compile it. But it *was* thorough.

The North Marshall Street inventory was a hefty sheaf of typewritten pages that carefully listed almost everything of note, a grab bag of items ranging from blood-stained clothing and chains to bags of bones and an aluminum pot with "a tan crusty residue around the rim." A footnote: "Analysis did not determine the identity of this tan material."

Investigators found several saws, including a jigsaw which failed to show traces of blood and a hacksaw that yielded paint samples matching flakes found on Lindsay's dismembered body. There were piles of used cotton swabs, a mayonnaise jar containing "what appeared to be onions" and a "thick slab of moldy, round, light-yellow, cream-colored cheese." Screwdrivers aplenty were found, along with a box of no-frills dog biscuits and—off in a corner— "a dirty, moldy, used condom."

Police spent days digging up Heidnik's yard, looking for more bodies. They never found any, but the search was not without its form of black humor.

With the curious crowding the streets and cheering encouragement, officers dug so many holes in the tiny yard it looked like an artillery target zone. One digger yelled and held up something that looked suspiciously like a human arm. It turned out to be a tree limb. Soon afterwards searchers uncovered a mass they thought was the remains of a human body. A frantic call went out for a medical examiner. After he examined it, he said it was simply a collection of refuse. Despite days of digging, all the searchers ever found, beside a few bones they immediately identified as belonging to Sandra Lindsay, was the skeleton of a cat.

All this poking, probing, and excavating was not without reason. When the captives gave statements to police, they said Heidnik had boasted of killing six women whose names he rattled off: Sandy, Debbie, Sallie, Jody, Marcie, and Carol. Two things added strength to this claim. At the time, no one had seen either of Heidnik's two former live-in women, Dorothy or Anjeanette Davidson, in years. Even more damning was a statement from Heidnik's former roommate, Tony Brown.

The day Heidnik was arrested, the thirty-one-year-old Brown wandered around to North Marshall Street to see what all the fuss was about. When a cop told him a guy named Gary Heidnik had been arrested for killing and torturing women, Brown volunteered that he was Heidnik's best friend and once lived in the house. They quickly whisked him off to headquarters for some detailed conversation. Eighteen hours later, according to the lawyer who later defended Heidnik, Brown was charged as an accomplice. In a statement leaked to the *Inquirer,* Brown embellished on Heidnik's crimes.

He said he had been with Heidnik in the summer of 1985 when Heidnik picked up a prostitute at the corner of Broad and Poplar, offering her a hundred dollars to come with him. Brown allegedly drove back to the house and went to bed, leaving Heidnik alone with the woman, whose name he did not know.

The next morning he went to the basement to put his dirty clothes in the washing machine. The woman was there. She was chained. He said she asked him to set her free. He refused, afraid of what Heidnik would do to him.

About a week later, Brown said, he had been out running errands, and when he returned he smelled a terrible odor. He went down into the basement and saw Heidnik cutting up her body. Later, he saw Heidnik bury the parts in the front yard.

Brown also told police he was present in the basement when his girlfriend, Sandra Lindsay, died. The tale he

told was similar to that of the victims. He said he saw
Heidnik trying to stuff bread in her mouth and she was
gagging, but he kept pushing it in. Then she died.

He and Heidnik then carried Lindsay upstairs. "I
could tell she wasn't breathing," he said. "I knew she was
dead." He added that he saw Heidnik having intercourse
with the corpse. He said he left when Heidnik dismembered the body.

There was only one thing wrong with the story. None
of the victims had ever seen Brown anywhere, much less
in the basement the day Lindsay died. There was another
minor problem too: Brown's IQ is only 75, barely above
the official level for mental deficiency. That does not
qualify him as incompetent for trial, however.

Despite these issues, Brown was charged with murdering Sandra Lindsay and with conspiracy, kidnapping,
and rape. He was thrown in jail and bail was set at
$50,000.

A month later, on May 1, Brown was released on his
own signature. The district attorney's office asked for his
release, saying he could aid the investigation of Heidnik
more if he were free than he could if he were kept in jail.
Two weeks after the Heidnik trial, the charges quietly
were dropped. Brown was a free man.

There was no chance, though, that Heidnik was going
to be released on bail. Never in a million years. Not under any circumstances short of divine intervention. He
was in jail to stay, and both he and the system were going
to have some adjusting to do. It was not going to prove
easy on either.

On March 25, within hours of his arrest, Heidnik was
attacked by another prisoner. He suffered a broken nose.
Following that incident, he was put in a special section of
the Philadelphia Detention Center and was allowed out
of his cell only two hours a day. Even then he was not

removed until all other inmates in the section had been locked down.

Despite these precautions, he was able within a few days to get alone long enough to try to kill himself. On April 2, his ninth day in jail, he went into the shower. While a guard was occupied trying to adjust the water temperature for Heidnik, he looped one end of his T-shirt over the shower nozzle, the other around his neck. He let his knees sag. When the guard glanced up, he summoned help. Heidnik was already unconscious. But they found him in time.

Many seasoned observers shook their heads. It was only going to be a matter of time before one or both of those episodes was repeated. Either he was going to try to kill himself or someone else was going to kill him. In addition to that, District Attorney Ronald Castille had said he planned to seek the death penalty. At the moment that seemed the least of Heidnik's worries.

"Tell me, Gary, what kind of seasoning did you use?"
—Defense Attorney A. Charles Peruto Jr.

Heidnik, staring hard at Peruto: "Man, you're crazy."

Chapter 24

Gary Heidnik led a queer life, no doubt about it. But his preoccupation with the women in his basement was not all-consuming. During that four-month period he did a number of things that would not be considered explicitly abnormal. For instance:

• Early in November he went to one of the city's largest Cadillac dealers, shopping for a new car. His previous one had been damaged in an accident. It didn't look as classy anymore. He knew precisely what he wanted: a De Ville with all the extras. "He wanted flash," sales manager David Pliner testified later. "He wanted everything you could put on an auto: a custom roof, continental kit, custom grill, wire wheels, the best tires—everything." He negotiated a trade-in on his other Cadillac and paid the difference in cash, a $12,240 check drawn on Merrill Lynch.

Introducing himself as a bishop in the United Church of the Ministers of God, Heidnik struck up an acquaintance with the salesman. Whenever he brought his car in for service, he and Pliner chatted about the stock market. Pliner gave him a stock tip that must have proved fruitful because he called Pliner a month later and expressed his gratitude.

• In December he returned to a VA psychiatric clinic in Philadelphia after a ten-month lapse in treatment. He was greeted warmly by some of the long-term patients and seemed touched by the response his return elicited. "Hey," he told Dr. Richard W. Hole, "they're glad to see me." He returned for group therapy regularly until the time of his arrest. Every time he left, he had in his pocket a supply of Thorazine which he was supposed to ingest. He apparently never did, because a considerable amount of the drug was found in his bedroom on North Marshall Street by police.

• In January there was the hearing before Judge Levin in family court. Although the judge was unsure how much Heidnik understood about the proceeding, he did not appear so deranged to cause concern. His wife Betty apparently did not think he acted abnormally either. At least she did not mention it to the judge.

Throughout this period, too, he was bringing other women into his house for sex. One of these was a long-time girlfriend who used to meet him every week. Another was Agnes Adams, who was not taken captive until her *second* time inside number 3520. Why did he capture her then and not the first time? Only Heidnik knows, and so far he hasn't volunteered that information. Police suspect that there were a number of others as well, streetwalkers and perhaps some of his friends from Elwyn.

The incidents with the other women, though, are instructive in one respect. They show that Heidnik was using some kind of selection process. He wasn't grabbing women willy-nilly off the street, taking them home and chaining them up. But his criteria are still a mystery. No one except he knows why he picked some and rejected others.

These glimpses into Heidnik's "worldly" persona are fascinating but not necessarily enlightening. In fact, they only cloud the issue. His lawyer spent long hours thinking about it. If a jury was going to have to question Heidnik's mental process, how could these seeming bouts of sanity be explained? Was mental illness something that could be turned on and off? Was it visible sometimes? Invisible at others? If someone was crazy, did they have to act crazy *all the time?* Was Gary Heidnik a nut or not? If he was a fruitcake, how could he sometimes act in an understandable way? If he was not, what could explain the perfectly atrocious and revolting things he did? Lawyers call it the "mad/bad line," the wavy, far-from-clear divider between someone being insane and just being vicious.

Insanity would be one of the two main prongs of Heidnik's case. To get off, to be found not guilty, was never considered a viable possibility. Three women were found in his basement, led there by a fourth. All of them unequivocally identified Heidnik as the man who had held them captive. His freezer was half full of body parts. Human bones were found in his yard. One of the former captives led investigators, like a steel ball to a magnet, to a second body. There was just too much evidence against him; he couldn't very well say "wrong guy."

The other main prong would be the argument that he did not *intend* to kill Sandra Lindsay and Deborah Dudley. Although District Attorney Ronald Castille had already decided to go for the death penalty, he could not ask for that, under Pennsylvania law, until he first won a conviction for first-degree murder. A conviction under anything less than first degree maxed out at life in prison. But Castille looked forward to the fight.

An outspoken law-and-order man, Castille fought as a Marine platoon commander in Vietnam. He left a leg there, on a dusty battlefield in the area known as I Corps. He had a reputation as a scrapper. Witness the fact that he was holding his office at all—a white Republican in a

city dominated by black Democrats. He had beaten a
black opponent in the election just a few months before,
and this was a good opportunity to show that he could
practice what he preached when he promised hard justice.

Like all major American cities, Philadelphia has a high
percentage of violent crime. As a rule, there is roughly a
murder a day in the city. There are arrests in about
eighty percent of them. So every year, somewhere around
three hundred murder charges are filed by the D.A.'s
office, give or take a dozen. Not all of those go to trial, of
course. And not all go to trial with the prosecutor seeking the death penalty. Usually there are twelve to fifteen
capital-punishment cases a year. Castille's office scored
about a sixty-six percent success rate. Death penalty
cases were far from rare, but there wasn't one every week
either.

For a while Castille even flirted with the idea of trying
the case himself. He decided against it when he saw how
strong the evidence was against Heidnik. In the end, he
knew, it would be primarily a battle of psychiatrists: the
Commonwealth's shrinks against the defense's shrinks.
That didn't sound like his kind of case. But it *did* sound
like a perfect case for one of his top assistants, a dedi-
cated worker down the hall named Charlie Gallagher.

Charles Gallagher, curiously, was into the case well
before Castille, before anyone else in the D.A.'s office, as
a matter of fact. He was home in bed, asleep, when his
phone rang soon after midnight on March 26, 1987. As
acting chief of the D.A.'s homicide division, the forty-
year-old Gallagher was accustomed to middle-of-the-
night phone calls. It was policy that either the chief or
assistant chief had to be notified when a charge of murder
was being contemplated, no matter what the hour. And
Gallagher had learned that murderers rarely respected a
public servant's work schedule. When he groped sleepily

for the phone, he suspected it was trouble. It was. Police Lieutenant James Hansen was on the line with some not so cheery news.

As Gallagher stifled a yawn, Hansen succinctly laid out the basics of the complaint against Gary Heidnik. He said he wanted a search warrant to get into Heidnik's house. He needed it pronto.

"I think that can be arranged," Gallagher said. After getting the warrant moving, the ADA went back to bed. He had an early day staring him in the face. He had a funeral to go to. A popular judge had died and he was being buried that morning.

As soon as he could break away from the services, Gallagher hurried to the office and called Hansen for a status report. It was about ten o'clock. The homicide detective said things were progressing smoothly, that everything had, indeed, been exactly as the complainant—a woman named Josefina Rivera—had outlined. While they were talking, she was leading another detective on a search of Wharton State Park across the Delaware River in New Jersey to see if she could find the spot where she saw Heidnik discard the second body.

As Hansen ran through some of the details for him, Gallagher felt his stomach tighten. To do all these things, Gallagher thought, this man Heidnik had to be more than crazy. He had to be evil.

Such thoughts loom large in Gallagher's mind. He grew up in a strict Catholic home. One of his sisters is a nun. He describes himself as a "strong" believer. Added to his religion-inspired perception was the fact that his childhood had not been a sheltered one. His father had been a cop for thirty-one years.

As more details emerged and the case against Heidnik began taking substance, Gallagher made up his mind that he wanted to try this one. If ever there was a case that screamed for the death penalty, this was it. The Catholic church's position might be different, but Gallagher was also a prosecutor, and in this case his public duty came first. Without a qualm—not even a flicker of hesitancy—he went to Castille and asked for permission to make the charge first-degree murder.

"The death penalty may not be a deterrent to crime," Gallagher said, "but it sure would deter Gary Heidnik."

Chapter 25

At the time the Heidnik story broke, A. Charles Peruto Jr. was trying a murder case in Lancaster, west of Philadelphia, deep in the heart of Amish country. During a break in the proceedings he routinely called his Philadelphia office and was put through to John Fognano, a cousin and a member of Peruto's small firm. Fognano was bubbling with excitement.

"You'll never guess who's been trying to reach you," he said excitedly. Before Peruto could respond, Fognano broke the news: "Gary Heidnik."

"Who?" said Peruto, not sure he had heard correctly.

"Gary Heidnik," Fognano repeated. "He wants to hire you. He wants you to represent him."

"Is this a joke?" Peruto asked in surprise. "How did he find out about me? Why me?"

When Peruto recounted this scenario he was being uncharacteristically modest. He was known throughout Philadelphia and southern New Jersey for two reasons: he was a high profile, shoot-from-the-lip criminal defense attorney who absolutely *loved* sensational cases, and he was the thirty-two-year-old son of one of the city's most colorful and respected defenders, A. Charles Peruto Sr. The father was Chuck, the son Chuck Jr. Chuck had a reputation for being clever, quick-witted, highly quotable, and a top-notch lawyer. Chuck Jr. had a reputation for being clever, quick-witted, and highly quotable. He was still working on the top-notch lawyer tag. It was not that he was a bad lawyer or even a mediocre one. But he was invariably compared to his father, and his father cast a long shadow.

Peruto—Chuck Jr. (he detests "Chuckie")—had read enough in the newspapers in the last few days to know that agreeing to represent Gary Heidnik would be as sensible as trying to juggle vials of nitroglycerine. The word in the legal community was that his father had advised him to keep away. But Chuck Jr. was curious.

"He says he got your name from the guy in the next cell," Fognano explained, mentioning a name to Peruto.

Of course, Peruto thought, so simple. A few weeks before, he had defended the cellmate on a murder charge and won a verdict of not guilty by reason of insanity. That explained how but not why. Anyway, even if Gary Heidnik did want him, he was not sure he wanted Gary Heidnik. He wasn't sure at all.

"You go see him," Peruto told Fognano after thinking it over. "You see if he's really the one who made the call and if you think he's serious. If that works out, I'll come see him as soon as I get back to Philadelphia." He was hooked, but he didn't want to admit it.

Two days later Peruto met with Heidnik in a common area in the center of a cell block at the Philadelphia Detention Center. When he walked in, Heidnik was waiting for him, clad in a standard orange prison jumpsuit. When he saw Peruto, Heidnik bounded to his feet and flipped a salute. "Mr. Peruto, I presume," he said.

Holy shit, thought Peruto, looking straight into the icy eyes of Gary Heidnik.

"Talk about weird experiences," Peruto recalled later. "Here we were, sitting in the middle of all these other cells, and the guys in there kept calling out to me, 'Hey, Chuck, come talk to me when you're through.' Apparently that impressed Heidnik. After a few minutes he said quietly, 'Boy, you're pretty popular around here.' "

The interview lasted for more than two hours. During that time, Heidnik sat quietly at the table that was bolted to the floor in the middle of the room and, in a soft, matter-of-fact voice, told the lawyer the story of his arrest and the events that led up to it. Peruto couldn't believe what he was hearing; it was just too grotesque. The whole time Heidnik was talking, Peruto grew increasingly disgusted. It was probably the worst story he'd ever heard. Finally, when Heidnik got to the part about how he had cooked Lindsay's body, Peruto couldn't handle it any longer. He responded in the way that is his second nature: he let his wise-guy persona take control.

"That really got to me," Peruto said. "I couldn't help myself. I had to ask a question."

Leaning over, Peruto whispered confidentially, "Tell me, Gary, what kind of seasoning did you use?"

There was a long silence. "He just stared at me," Peruto said. "Then he answered, very distinctly, 'Man, you're crazy.' The way he said that made the hair on my neck stand up. I thought, 'Oh Chuck, you've gotten yourself into it this time. This is going to be a real experience.' "

An attorney who makes his living defending criminals cannot always be particular about his clients. He figures he is automatically going to get a high percentage of riff-raff no matter how picky he tries to be. Referrals—and getting their names in the newspapers—are what keep defense attorneys in business. Given the nature of the profession, the jailhouse grapevine is a crackerjack advertising medium. It doesn't always bring in the crème de la crème, but then again, the percentage of crème de la crème that gets charged with gruesome crimes is relatively low.

Defense attorneys, at least those who do it day in and

day out, get a lot of clients of the type most people wouldn't sit next to on a bus. But there are limits, and Peruto was not sure Heidnik didn't exceed the parameters. Defending Heidnik would get his name in the papers for sure, but he was not altogether convinced he needed the publicity that much. The crimes Heidnik was accused of committing were downright repulsive. Just talking about them made most people queasy. But defense attorneys, in that sense, are not ordinary people. Where others see sleaze, a good defense attorney sees challenge. When others think of senseless violence, defense attorneys think of motivation. *What* made the accused commit that violent act often is more important in the courtroom than the violence itself. There is always a reason, even if the reason is not readily apparent; even if the reason is insanity. The defense attorney's task is to make a jury see the mitigating circumstances, make them understand that their client had a basis for doing what he did.

If a jury can see logic behind behavior, even twisted logic, it becomes comprehensible. When others envision hopelessness, defense attorneys see hope. They also see dollar signs and headlines. But there are limits. No defense attorney builds a reputation by consistently standing up next to losers. No one is going to rush out to hire you if the last three or four people you defended were presented open-ended reservations at Graterford, Pennsylvania's main penitentiary. On the surface, Heidnik's case looked unwinnable. If ever there had been a born loser, Heidnik was one. If ever there had been a series of repulsive crimes, this was it. If ever there was a case in which the police had caught someone redhanded, it was Heidnik's. At that point neither Peruto nor anyone else would have said that Heidnik had even the slimmest of chances of escaping the death penalty.

On one hand, Peruto was intrigued; on the other, repelled. There are better ways to make a buck, he figured. Still . . .

The way to settle it for sure, he decided, the way to keep from having to make a moral and professional issue out of it, was to let economics be the first hurdle. Peruto figured he would set an outlandish fee, one so high that Heidnik would immediately back off.

"I'll defend you," Peruto told him, "but it's going to cost you a hundred thousand dollars."

"Okay," Heidnik replied without hesitation.

"Jesus," Peruto said to himself.

"I wanted to say," he admitted later in an interview, " 'Gary, I'm not a hundred-thousand-dollar lawyer. I usually charge a flat ten thousand fee for a homicide.' "

But then, this wasn't any ordinary homicide.

Chapter 26

Chuck Peruto didn't have to wait long to see just how unordinary it was. On this Thursday, as April was sliding into May, he made his first major appearance with his client. It was a traumatic experience.

The occasion was a preliminary hearing, a procedure fixed by law to formally determine if there is probable cause to hold an accused for trial. In Heidnik's case it was superfluous, but the law said it had to be done. To Peruto's consternation and Gallagher's delight, it was a showcase for the district attorney's office, because it gave the Commonwealth a chance to brag about what a solid case it had against Gary Heidnik. From start to finish it was strictly a prosecutorial event.

The formal charges against Peruto's client were murder, kidnapping, rape, aggravated assault, involuntary deviate sexual intercourse, plus indecent exposure, false imprisonment, unlawful restraint, simple assault, making terroristic threats, recklessly endangering another person, indecent assault, criminal solicitation, possession and abuse of a corpse. The latter charge was defined as a crime in which Heidnik "unlawfully did treat a corpse in a way that he knew would outrage ordinary family sensibilities."

Waiting in Room 675 in City Hall were seven witnesses: the four former captives, a sister of one of the
murder victims, and two medical examiners for the city.
Also present were Municipal Court Judge Charles Margiotti Jr.; the prosecutor, Assistant District Attorney
Charles Gallagher; Peruto and, of course, Gary Heidnik.

With a nod from Judge Margiotti, the parade began.

Lisa Thomas was the third woman to join Heidnik's
harem, but she was first on the stand. In a steady voice
she told the silent crowd how she was picked up, how
Heidnik enticed her with food and presents, how he had
sex with her and then took her captive. Not a sound
could be heard when she explained how Heidnik had re-
inforced his domination over her by forcing her to perform oral-genital sex in front of the others.

Thomas' tale was concise and unemotional, accurate
yet withdrawn, a perfect warm-up for Josefina Rivera.

If Thomas was impressive, Rivera was spectacular. In
a flat, detached voice which gave her narrative even more
power, Rivera bombarded the crowd with a tale so horri-
ble, so detailed, that even veteran court watchers were
moved.

In the beginning her story paralleled Thomas', differ-
ing only in the fact that she had been the first captive. She
also had been hoodwinked, she said, forcibly captured
and horribly mistreated. But when she got to the part of
how Lindsay died, the story took a direction of its own.
Truth, indeed, had proved stranger than fiction.

When Lindsay had collapsed that second time and
Heidnik came down the stairs, she said she could feel his
anger. "He lifted her left wrist and let it fall." There was
no response. He uncuffed her and she fell in a heap.
"Then he kicked her into the hole and felt for her pulse.
When there wasn't one, he said she had choked on a
piece of bread."

Five weeks after Sandra Lindsay's death, Rivera said,

it was Deborah Dudley's turn. On March 18 Heidnik was punishing Thomas, Dudley, and Jacquelyn Askins. He decided to give them electric shock.

Heidnik ruled the women with an iron hand, she said, and he expected to be obeyed. When he told her to help punish the other three, she never even considered telling him no.

While Heidnik watched and chuckled, Rivera dragged a garden hose over to a hole in which the captives were kept and filled it with water. Thomas, Dudley, and Askins were already in the pit. When the hole was full, Heidnik plugged a white extension cord into an outlet across the room. Then he plugged a second cord into that. At his direction, Rivera touched the wires onto Dudley's chain. All three of them screamed. They then grew silent. Heidnik thought the cord had burned up, so he dashed upstairs to get another one. Askins yelled that Dudley was dead.

"There's nothing wrong with Debbie," said Heidnik. But when he walked over and peered into the pit, he saw Dudley was limp and her face was in the water.

Rivera told how Heidnik had forced her to write a confession admitting to Dudley's death. " 'That's so you will be guilty too,' " she said he told her.

Rivera's testimony that it was she who had held the electrical cords when Dudley died was not lost on Peruto. When his turn for cross-examination came, he probed Thomas about Rivera's participation, not only in Dudley's electrocution but in other torture sessions conducted in the basement.

Rivera frequently beat the other captives, Thomas admitted, both when Heidnik was there and when he wasn't. "She enjoyed it." She was the boss of the basement, Thomas said. "She would beat us on our bottoms and on our legs with a stick, laughing the whole time."

According to Thomas, it also was Rivera who gave Heidnik the idea of using electric shock.

Thomas' assertions, however, were contradicted by Askins, who swore that Rivera never beat them unless Heidnik ordered her to.

Nevertheless, Askins added, Rivera *had* been a snitch. She said that at one point all of them agreed they would try to overpower Heidnik and escape. But before they could execute their plan, Rivera tipped off Heidnik. As a result, all of them except Rivera were punished severely. Rivera, on the other hand, was rewarded. "[She]and Gary would go out and then come back and tell us what a good time they had. And then they would laugh about it," said Askins.

When asked what possible motive Heidnik could have had in this incredible escapade, all of the victims agreed: he had his mind set on getting them all pregnant and raising the babies in the cellar.

"He wanted ten girls and as many babies as possible before he died," said Askins.

"He wanted me to get pregnant because he would like to have a lot of kids running around in the basement," confirmed Thomas.

Since the fourth captive, Agnes Adams, was only in the basement for one night, there was nothing substantial she could add to the testimony of the other three.

But it had been a wrenching day, an emotionally draining experience. By the time the two witnesses from the medical examiner's office took the stand, their appearance was almost anticlimatic.

Dr. Robert L. Catherman's testimony was exceedingly brief. Basically, he confirmed that Dudley had died of electrical shock. But his colleague, Dr. Paul Hoyer, was considerably more forthcoming. It was Hoyer who had examined the body parts found in Heidnik's freezer.

Painstakingly, ADA Gallagher led Hoyer through the

steps that led to the discovery, beginning with his arrival at the house on North Marshall Street.

"Did you observe anything peculiar in the kitchen?" Gallagher asked.

"Yes, I did," responded Hoyer.

"And what was that, Doctor?"

"Two items. First of all, there was a white refrigerator in the kitchen. And located in the freezer compartment of the refrigerator were several white . . . bagged parcels, as you would perhaps wrap up a piece of meat to keep it in the freezer, double wrapped in a white plastic bag. One of these bags had been previously opened. And I looked inside this bag and I believe I found two human forearms."

"And what did you do? Were there other items wrapped similarly in the refrigerator?"

"There were other items wrapped similarly in the refrigerator," Hoyer confirmed. "I removed an additional parcel, opened that parcel, and found what appeared to be a human upper arm."

"And were there any other items found in the refrigerator?" Gallagher queried.

"Yes. There were other parcels found in the refrigerator, which were subsequently brought to my office for examination."

Gallagher and Hoyer interrupted each other, both trying to talk at the same time. Then Hoyer resumed.

". . . in sum, there were two forearms, one upper arm, two knees, and two segments of thigh. Each of these pieces had . . . the bone end had been cut apparently with a saw. And the skin and muscle, soft tissue, was still on the bone." Twenty-four pounds in all, it was determined.

Had he examined the oven? Gallagher wanted to know. Certainly, said Hoyer. "There were things in the oven that had been cooked and cooked and cooked for hours."

* * *

The room was abuzz. If this crime was not the most gruesome in recent Philadelphia history, no one could think of a worse one. If Gallagher's purpose had been to build public opinion against Heidnik, he had certainly succeeded.

There was one problem, however, which became more evident in retrospect. It was that Gallagher's presentation may have been *too* expansive. All the Commonwealth had to do was present enough evidence to justify holding Heidnik for trial, but Gallagher went far beyond this. Some shrewd court watchers mumbled that Gallagher exposed too much of the Commonwealth's case. This gave the defense a good look at what evidence the prosecution had, *plus* it locked in the four witnesses to testimony they might give at the trial. They could elaborate on their testimony, but if they tried to deviate, it threw them open to impeachment.

"Josefina Rivera would have been quite sufficient," said one lawyer with a close eye on the case.

Chapter 27

While most of the focus was on the criminal charges against Heidnik, a different drama was being played out in the city's civil courts. Eventually it would become an issue in the criminal case as well.

As soon as the captives learned how much money Heidnik had in the bank, they filed suit against their former captor, seeking to dip into the half-million dollars he was reported to have tucked away in an account at Merrill Lynch. But Heidnik contended the money did not belong to him but to his church, the United Church of the Ministers of God.

Not everyone agreed with this distinction. Some claimed the church was just a front, that Heidnik *was* the church and its money was really his money. Before this issue could be settled, however, it had to be determined which court had jurisdiction, state or federal. *That* would be the first major battle to determine the legitimacy of Heidnik's church and the distribution of funds.

On April 6, four days after Heidnik tried to hang himself, attorneys for Lisa Thomas filed a petition in the civil division of Common Pleas Court asking that the church's assets be frozen and a conservator appointed. Judge Samuel M. Lehrer immediately complied with the first part of the request. But he waited fourteen days, until April 20, to name a conservator.

One hour and forty-five minutes before Lehrer got around to announcing his choice as conservator, Heidnik filed a Chapter Eleven bankruptcy petition in federal court. That document listed three of the surviving captives plus the estates of the two murdered captives as creditors. All told, the document noted, they were seeking several million dollars in damages. An incidental creditor, interestingly enough, was the City of Philadelphia, asking $6,800 in back child-support payments.

Significantly, the filing of bankruptcy set the stage for the battle over jurisdiction. Judge Lehrer, of the Common Pleas Court, was determined not to surrender. In an April 27 ruling he ordered his newly-named conservator to seize the church's assets, including the half-million-dollar Merrill Lynch account, plus a local bank account containing $16,000, a 1987 Cadillac valued at $34,000, and a 1971 Rolls-Royce.

He also used that occasion to launch a bitter attack against the organization, labeling it a "sham" and a church that "exists in name only." Angrily, Lehrer made it clear he thought the church was a fabrication devised by Heidnik solely to evade taxes. "Do you have a church program?" he demanded. "A schedule of Sunday services or Saturday services? Do you have a membership list? Books? Pamphlets? Prayer guides?" These were rhetorical questions; he never waited for answers. His indignation was barreling along like a sixteen-wheeler without brakes.

"I find that it is in the public interest that such an entity be found to be what it is," Lehrer raged. "The mere thought that this is a church is offensive and an insult to all persons in the community. Further, it is also offensive and an insult to the sensibilities of the victims and their families . . . that such crimes could be perpetrated . . . in the name and the guise of something called a church."

Lehrer's position was not unique. At first even Peruto was ready to believe the church was simply a con. "But after I took the case, people started calling me saying they had been members and they wanted to know if someone was still holding services. I was amazed. The more I found out about it, the more I was convinced it wasn't a tax dodge."

Dr. Clancy McKenzie, a psychiatrist who spent more than a hundred hours with Heidnik after his arrest, also vehemently denied accusations that it was a mock operation.

While some were terribly uncomfortable in thinking of the church as a church, there also were some who were equally uncomfortable with Lehrer's presumption of jurisdiction. The day following Lehrer's ruling, Tuesday, April 28, U.S. District Judge David A. Scholl held a hearing to determine if the case should be in Lehrer's province at all or in the federal courts. Three weeks later, on May 19, he handed down *his* decision. He said *he*— not Judge Lehrer—had control.

In a twenty-page decision, Scholl said the jurisdiction shifted when the Chapter Eleven petition was filed. At that point the federal bankruptcy court became "all-powerful and exempt from compromise."

Although he thought Judge Lehrer's anger at "what he believed was the sacrilegious hypocrisy of cloaking the financial support of [Heidnik's] activities in the name of a church strictly for the purposes of tax evasion" was "totally appropriate," he nevertheless slammed Lehrer's conclusion that the church was a sham. In his words, the state court judge's decision was "legally void."

Judge Scholl also appointed two trustees, one for Heidnik and one for the church, to administer the estate.

Those proceedings had one very important immediate

effect on the criminal case. When the church's assets were frozen, Peruto saw his promised $100,000 fee go down the tube. To his credit, he refused to submit a bill for time spent and walk away. Soon afterwards he was formally appointed Heidnik's lawyer, so he picked up exactly where he left off. Except this time it was at the rather unsensational fee of sixty dollars an hour. Despite the pay cut, he resolved to stick with his client.

Chapter 28

May 14, 1987

Five days before Judge Scholl's ruling in federal court, Heidnik was called into Common Pleas Court for still another proceeding, called a status hearing. It would be his final court appearance until jury selection got under way.

Heidnik hobbled into the courtroom and came face to face with Judge Charles L. Durham, a suave black man who also served as the court's calendar judge. With his ankles chained together and his hands cuffed in front of him with a chain running to a thick leather belt, Heidnik looked like Houdini being prepared for an escape trick. As a sheriff's department officer reached over to uncuff Heidnik, the officer was overcome by the drama of the situation; his hands shook so badly he couldn't fit the tiny key into the lock. Heidnik watched the white-shirted officer's performance with interest. As the officer fumbled around, Heidnik turned to Peruto and softly whispered, "Something's wrong with this man." It was the longest sentence he would utter during the entire proceeding, and the only one that indicated he knew what was going on.

Peruto explained to a grim-faced Durham that his client would not be testifying.

That was all right, Durham replied, all he wanted to do was ask Heidnik a few easy questions to make sure he understood where he was and what was happening to him.

Heidnik, his hands now free, ripped off a military salute to the judge. Standing at a loose parade rest, he cast his eyes down, intently eyeing the floor. Occasionally his head twitched.

Judge Durham looked him up and down. "Mr. Heidnik!" he called.

Heidnik popped to attention and saluted again.

"Mr. Heidnik—" Durham began.

"Yes, sir," Heidnik snapped.

"Do you know where you are?"

"Yes, sir."

"How old are you?"

"Yes, sir."

"Do you speak English?"

"Yes, sir."

"Are you going to the moon today?"

"Don't answer that," Peruto whispered in his ear.

Heidnik remained silent.

When asked if he wanted to plead guilty or not guilty, Peruto answered for him: "Not guilty, your honor."

Frustrated, Durham accepted his plea and moved to the next case.

Later, in a brief hallway news conference, Peruto exonerated Heidnik for not speaking, saying he had been under his command to keep quiet. He planned to plead his client insane, and he did not want a prosecution psychiatrist to be able to use anything he might say in court later as evidence to damage his case.

Afterwards, Peruto got down to more mundane tasks: the blizzard of paperwork that surrounds cases such as this.

On May 22, eight days after the status hearing—just long enough for all the salacious tidbits to be displayed and debated in the media—Peruto requested a change of venue. Media coverage had been "highly prejudicial and inflammatory and in deprivation of the defendant's rights to a fair and impartial trial and his rights to due process," he claimed. "The details, events, and facts surrounding the matters relating to this case are now generally so well known to the citizens and inhabitants of this county that a fair and unbiased jury would be impossible to select."

He also filed several other motions, dealing with the search of Heidnik's house and the seizure of his property, but it was pretty standard legal maneuvering that would have been expected in almost any significant criminal case. The most important issue was the request for a change of venue. Wisely, Judge Durham decided not to rule on that until a trial date had been set. No one knew it then, but that was even more distant than the most pessimistic observers believed. After all, Peruto had only started to romp through his repertoire of motions.

Chapter 29

April 4, 1988

For everyone, except possibly Gary Heidnik, the previous eleven months had gone by in a blur. The case was out of the headlines and off the six o'clock news. Time and the vagaries of the news business had seen to that.

When the details of Heidnik's crimes were made public, hard-nosed cops and toughened murder buffs said they could not remember incidents as grisly as those attributed to the man from North Marshall Street. Then, in less than five months, they had another case that almost overshadowed Heidnik's.

On August 9, 1987, a steamy Sunday, police got a call from an angry resident of a disreputable northside ghetto who said blood was dripping into his apartment from the cubicle upstairs. Probably nothing less would have prompted such a call. The building involved was so loathsome that its occupants, lacking even running water and indoor plumbing, defecated in buckets and dumped the contents in the trash-filled backyard.

When police arrived, they were almost overcome by the smell. Donning gas masks, they forced their way into a back bedroom whose door had been nailed shut. In the room were remains of five women. The body of a sixth woman was found wrapped in sheets inside a closet in the room, which also had been nailed shut. Still one more body was found, part of it on the roof and part in the basement of a neighboring building. A few days later a retarded twenty-nine-year-old black man built like a tight end surrendered. Harrison "Marty" Graham said he began killing the women the previous winter, the same time Heidnik was holding his captives less than two miles away. Graham said he lured the women with offers of drugs, then strangled them during intercourse.

He also confessed to being a necrophiliac. Until he could no longer stand the odor, he said, he would periodically return to the bodies for sex.

The details of Graham's revolting escapades made Philadelphians temporarily forget about Heidnik, who had been left to vegetate in a psychiatric ward while Peruto and Gallagher built their files for the trial. Officially, the proceeding was to start on the first Monday in April. Of course, it did not start then. Nor would it for many weeks, as a matter of fact. But everyone had to go through the motions. The entire cast, minus only Heidnik, that had been in Judge Durham's courtroom the previous May, was back in Room 613 on April 4.

Peruto and Gallagher stood shoulder to shoulder in the small chamber, waiting for Durham to formally assign the case to a judge who would preside at the trial. Except for the fact that both men were roughly the same height—about five feet eight—the two lawyers could hardly have been more different.

Peruto was a dandy with a taste for custom-made suits and shirts, gold cuff links, and fancy shoes. He wore a beard, which was short and immaculately groomed. His hair was styled just a tad longer than the current fashion and frozen with hair spray. He had a weightlifter's torso and a subtle arrogance of bearing. In profile he resembled Burt Reynolds. Like the movie star, he was not unaware of his physicality and the image he presented to admirers

—the younger and the more shapely, the better—who flocked to the courtroom to see him in action.

Gallagher, in contrast, was as unpretentious as a Naugahyde sofa. He dressed in off-the-rack suits in gray, grayer, and black, with pure white shirts and red foulard ties. His shoes were drill-field practical. If he was growing a little thick around the middle, it didn't seem to bother him; he simply substituted suspenders for a confining belt. He wore his hair cut short, in the military style, with his graying sideburns chopped off at mid-ear. He wouldn't have known a can of hair spray if it fell in his lap. His rimless spectacles could have been Navy issue, the frames stamped with a bold USN rather than YSL. He looked like a chubby Ollie North.

Durham, wearing the hat of calendar judge, wasted no time. Trying the Heidnik case, he announced, would be Lynne M. Abraham. It would be up to her, he added, to set a date for jury selection and to rule on all future motions, including Peruto's request for change of venue and a request he had just filed to force the prosecution's psychiatrist, Dr. Robert Sadoff, to provide a list of the cases in which he had testified.

Suddenly, the hearing was finished. It took less than ten minutes. The reporters who crowded the room went away without much to report, but with some research to do. They all scurried to their computers to search their electronic libraries to see what they could find on the new character in the continuing drama: Lynne Abraham. What was the story on this female judge?

Chapter 30

The story on Lynne Abraham was that she was, by her own admission, one "tough cookie." A heavyset, slightly masculine woman who wore her salt-and-pepper hair cut short and brushed back over her ears, she was a formidable veteran of both the Philadelphia court system and Philadelphia politics.

When she graduated from Temple University Law School a generation ago, there were not many lawyer jobs available for women in public-service agencies, so she went to work with the U.S. Department of Housing and Urban Development. Secretly, she was searching for a way to get into the courtroom.

She devoted her days to HUD and her nights to graduate classes at Temple. Soon she became friendly with one of her instructors, who happened to be District Attorney Arlen Specter's top deputy. The man introduced Abraham to Specter, and he offered her a job. Her main reservation had been that she would be assigned to juvenile court, but she negotiated an agreement with her new employer to work magistrate's court instead. That would do, she figured, until she could find a way to get to where she really wanted to be: the homicide division, prosecuting cases in Common Pleas Court. It didn't take her long.

Once she got there, she quickly won the respect of the

other ADAs and the judges for her knowledge of the law and her aggressiveness. Her acceptance among defense attorneys was more guarded because she was hard to beat. She was a perfectionist, and the job became a passion. Take forensics, for example. She became preoccupied with the basics of the cases she was prosecuting, and decided the best way to get a thorough grounding in her cases was to start at the beginning. Much to the surprise of the city's medical examiners, she began turning up at autopsies. It helped her, she said, when she got into court. Knowing exactly how a victim had died—and why —gave her an edge when she asked a jury to come down heavy on the murderer. She showed no mercy to defense attorneys or their clients. She seldom compromised; "plea bargain" was a phrase that made her stomach turn.

In quick order she became known as an obdurate, relentless prosecutor.

Her name came to the attention of Mayor Frank L. Rizzo, who was having personnel problems in his administration and was looking for someone from the outside to come in and clean up the mess. He offered her a job as head of the Redevelopment Authority. It was Rizzo who hung the "tough cookie" nickname on her and bragged that if anybody could erase the corruption in the agency, she could. Five years after taking her first case, Abraham left the district attorney's office. She would never step into a courtroom again except as judge.

The honeymoon with Rizzo, however, was brief. Within a year the two were disagreeing vehemently. After fifteen months he fired her, claiming developers didn't want to work with her because she was too arrogant. *She* said he wanted to get rid of her because she wouldn't hire his buddies or agree to turn a blind eye to procedures involving certain contracts.

Wiser for her initial foray into politics, she looked for another way back into the courtroom. In 1975 she was elected the city's first female Municipal Court judge.

Four years later she ran for a job with more authority, a seat on the bench in the Common Pleas Court. During that campaign she took a page from Mayor Rizzo's book; she won public support by standing on street corners handing out "tough cookies."

Although she was back in the courtroom, politics was still pulling her. In 1985, at the age of forty-four, she feinted toward a run for district attorney but backed out when support she thought she was going to get from Mayor W. Wilson Goode dissolved. In that case the Democratic black power structure decided a black man would make a better candidate than a white woman. But the man they put up was trounced by Republican Ronald Castille, a hard-charging former Marine who left a leg in Vietnam.

The forces that drove Abraham to be an absorbed, unyielding prosecutor and a potential candidate for political office became apparent when she took over the Heidnik trial. Her instincts as an inflexible ADA were still there, coupled with a tendency to be pedantic. During jury selection particularly she drove the defense attorney, Peruto, to distraction, and though he would never admit it, perhaps Gallagher as well, by repeatedly interrupting their questioning of potential jurors, called "veniremen" in legal parlance. "Let me rephrase that," was one of her favorite lines, a phrase she repeated whenever she thought one of the attorneys had not been explicit enough in his grilling. "Let me put that another way," was another of her favorites. Or, fixing the venireman with a steely gaze that was sure to intimidate, she would say, just after one of the lawyers finished a query, "Don't answer that! This is what Mr. Peruto [or Mr. Gallagher] meant."

It wasn't so much that her interpretations were inaccurate, it was just that they seemed to be superfluous, almost always wordy and theatrical, and at times even condescending. In many cases the potential jurors appeared to understand all too well what the attorney was asking but of course, were in no position to point this out to Judge Abraham.

When Abraham chose to, she exhibited a robust sense of humor; she could also send everyone running for cover, particularly members of the media to whom she devoted special attention. It often seemed she held reporters in contempt, though at other times she seemed bent on making a good impression. Perhaps she doesn't like the press (although her husband is a local radio personality), but she is certainly shrewd enough to recognize its usefulness, particularly if she has her eye on something higher than a seat on the Common Pleas bench. The word among insiders at the time of the Heidnik trial was that she had written off the possibility of seeking the district attorney's job and was directing her efforts instead to a possible campaign for a spot on the state supreme court. If that were true, what better launch vehicle than a trial guaranteed to take an exceptional share of the headlines? She would not be the first jurist whose career was helped by presiding over a sensational case. Nor would she be the last.

Chapter 31

May 16, 1988

Gary Heidnik was not only out of mind, he was out of sight as well. Except for his lawyer, a few shrinks and prison personnel, no one had seen him for a year. But that quickly changed. On a cool, overcast Monday in the middle of May, twelve months and two days after his last public appearance, he sprang—or rather, he shuffled—back into public view. When the heavily bolted door in Judge Abraham's courtroom swung open, a dozen or so reporters and a handful of spectators strained to catch a glimpse of the man who, despite Marty Graham, still held a lock on grisly crime in Philadelphia.

As they watched in open-mouthed amazement, a wraithlike Gary Heidnik skated into the room, slowly sliding his feet across the floor. He moved like a cross-country skier who had unexpectedly run out of snow. His scuffed, ankle-high black boots may have been made of lead or attached by a powerful force to the room's stained, green carpet. Left . . . right . . . left . . . right, slowly he lurched along. Reporters looked at one another and raised their eyebrows. "Is this Gary Heidnik?"

In the intervening months Heidnik's reputation as a crazed woman killer had grown. The Madman of Marshall Street had taken on monstrous proportions. He had become the *infamous* Gary Heidnik. In the myth he was seven feet tall; brawny; defiant; scornful; a walking stick of dynamite. But the reality was something else. What the world was expecting was not what it got.

The *old* Gary Heidnik had a reputation in his neighborhood as something of a neat dresser, even if he did have a thing for cowhide. In the past one of his favorite articles of clothing was a sleeveless black-leather vest. And he absolutely *loved* the fringed buckskin jacket he was wearing when he was carted off to jail. In Philadelphia you saw a lot of Gary in that jacket because the local TV stations liked to show those film clips every time there was a development in the story. The deputies who guarded him, however, hoped they *never* saw that jacket again. They complained it was indelibly saturated with the stench of burning flesh.

It was said on North Marshall Street that Heidnik always dressed tidily, even if he was only going into the garage to work on his cars. Apparently, incarceration had influenced him to turn over a new sartorial leaf. When he stumbled out of the holding cell passageway behind the courtroom for the beginning of jury selection —a process known in the trade as voir dire; in Latin, "to say the truth"—he certainly gave no hint that he ever took pride in his attire. He was an emaciated wretch in a clown costume.

His khaki pants were clean and neatly pressed, but they were at least two sizes too large. They bunched at the waist, bagged in the rear, flared in the thigh and dragged the floor. He wore a dark blue, wool, navy watchcoat. It was fully buttoned, but it was not known if that was in deference to the weather or because it was his established psychiatric pattern to overdress. Beneath the coat, his shirt of choice was the same faded-black Hawaiian number with the purple orchids and bright green leaves that he had worn the year before at his arraignment. Maybe it had been washed in the interim. Maybe it hadn't. Later, during the trial, Peruto had to get a court order to make him change his shirt and take a shower.

In fairness, his wardrobe selection was limited. All of his own garments, including his treasured buckskin jacket, were still being held by police as evidence. The man in charge of the jail's used-clothing room had become his haberdasher. Obviously they weren't good friends.

But there was more to Heidnik's mildly outlandish garb than that. Peruto *wanted* him to look scruffy. Like a street person. Like a nut. If you're a lawyer building an insanity defense, you don't want your client coming to court looking like he just stopped off at Brooks Brothers for a trial suit. Peruto helped pick the clothing. He told Heidnik to shuffle. To look vacant and disconnected. To salute him each morning. It was part of the game. There was more to being a defense lawyer, Peruto insisted, than appearing in court and arguing motions.

Of course, Peruto got more than a little help from prison doctors, who kept Heidnik under control with three hundred milligrams a day of Thorazine.

One thing that was not faked, though, was Heidnik's physical condition. It was deplorable. Anyone watching the film clips of his arrest saw a not unhandsome man. *That* Heidnik had a short, neatly groomed beard. A barbered coif. A straight nose and a well-filled form. Generally a healthy-looking specimen. *This* Heidnik was about thirty pounds lighter. His neck had grown long and scrawny. His arms were matchsticks. His handcuff-encircled wrists were bony and had a bluish cast. But the big difference was the hair. *This* Heidnik had not cut his hair for fourteen months, and it hung in long, greasy tangles to his shoulders. Obviously he had not shampooed it in days, perhaps weeks. His beard, streaked with gray, tumbled untrimmed and uncombed to his chest. His nose was humped and bent off center, a souvenir of an attack by other inmates the day of his arrest. In short, he looked like a wreck. Just like Peruto wanted him to.

One thing remained unchanged, however: his eyes. Blue-gray aggies as cold as a Philadelphia winter, they were still wild, still angry. "Creepy eyes," his lawyer called them. Charlie Manson eyes. A fanatic's eyes.

Heidnik's appearance had an unreal feel to it. A spooky feel. But it fit the venue. Gary Heidnik might not be your usual, everyday accused murderer, but then the building in which his trial was being held, Philadelphia's City Hall, was not your usual, everyday brick-and-glass county courthouse.

Chapter 32

City Hall. Style. History. Nobility. Degeneration. Squalor. Take your pick; they all apply.

Patterned after the New Louvre, in the style known as French-Victorian, the building was erected in the 1880s in what was then the city's central square. Today it sits all alone at the center of a huge traffic circle, smack in the middle of the city's business district, rising out of a sea of cars like a man-made Gibraltar. The first seven floors are constructed in a huge block, which is divided into work space. Atop the block is a graceful tower capped by a statue of William Penn, the city's founder and the state's namesake. From the ground to the top of Billy Penn's hat it is 491 feet, forty stories give or take. Until 1987, when a sixty-one story skyscraper known as One Liberty Place was erected nearby, it was the city's tallest building. Although bested in height, it has lost none of its majesty.

It is a pity that the building's grandeur is only skin deep. Inside, the building is no longer so grand at all. The corridors are as wide as some of the surrounding old streets, and just about as dingy. The linoleum floors are cracked and pocked by cigarette burns; permanently stained by mysterious, corrosive liquids. Discarded food wrappers, crumbled coffee cups, empty soda cans, and old newspapers pile up in the halls, which are home to criminals and police alike.

Occasionally they are used for other things as well. One day just before the trial, when a persistent heat wave discouraged outdoor running, a jogger wearing a blue tank top and gray Reeboks determinedly did his laps around the sixth-floor rectangle. The circuit is about a third of a mile.

The corridors are lined with tall windows, a delight for those who appreciate good design. Unfortunately, they look almost exclusively inward, opening onto empty airshafts and undeveloped courtyards strewn with rubbish and broken furniture.

If the corridors seem bad, the stairways are worse. Much worse. Although designed to angle elegantly around a broad open area to give a feeling of spaciousness, they have deteriorated into dark, evil-smelling passageways. When the early morning cleaning crews come in, the first thing they tackle are the stairwells, where they commonly find puddles of urine and piles of excrement.

City Hall's deterioration is not entirely the result of a lack of concern. The building simply is overused and underfunded. It is a working building, not a museum. There are courtrooms for eighty judges in the building. The criminal division of the Common Pleas Court, the largest user, has almost fifty judges and hundreds of attendants: law clerks, calendar clerks, minute clerks, recorders, secretaries, receptionists, telephone answerers, bailiffs, criers, stenographers, court reporters, and sergeants-at-arms. Each year some thirteen thousand criminal proceedings are held in the building, including about three hundred fifty murder trials.

Each day some two hundred fifty prisoners pass through City Hall's southwest portal, the traditional depository and pickup point. Their transportation isn't fancy: a large brown or blue school bus with heavy wire over the windows and an interior partitioned into a large cage. But Heidnik got special treatment. As a potential suicide, he almost always traveled alone, either in a van or station wagon. However, that special treatment ended at the portal. Once there, he marched to an elevator like all the prisoners and got an express to the seventh floor, where the holding cells are located.

Heidnik was usually mixed in with other prisoners in one of the fifty-man cells. Commonly, he wiggled his way into a corner and either read from the pocket-sized New Testament he carried in a smudged manila envelope or slept until it was time for him to be taken downstairs to Room 653, Judge Abraham's bailiwick.

—

Room 653 is somewhat infamous around the courthouse; it has its own little spot in the building's history books. What makes it unusual is an event that happened there on August 18, 1986. Judge Lynne Abraham was on the bench, and in the defendant's chair, instead of Gary Heidnik, was a thirty-nine-year-old unemployed construction worker named Robert McPeake, charged, as was Heidnik, with rape. For five days a jury had been listening to testimony in his case. McPeake had an earlier conviction for the same crime and knew if he was found guilty again, he could expect no mercy at sentencing. When the jury came back, the verdict was against him. Exercising his option, McPeake's attorney asked that the jurors be polled. One by one they stood and individually confirmed that they had judged the defendant guilty. McPeake, in the meantime, sat stiffly at the defense table, shooting nervous glances around the room. Suddenly, just as the penultimate juror rose to authenticate the decision, McPeake leaped from his chair and dashed across the room. Raising his hands over his head like a diver on the high board, he leaped out a window, plummeting six floors to his death. After the courtroom had been cleared, a still-shocked Abraham shook her head. "I've been in court for a lot of years," she said sadly, "but nothing could have prepared me for this."

McPeake taught Abraham a lesson. When it came time for Gary Heidnik to make his appearance, the judge wasn't taking any chances. When he materialized, his hands were cuffed securely behind him. At each shoulder was a burly deputy. In front of the window through which McPeake exited was an oscillating fan on a stand. Since it was never turned on, it was assumed that its function was to serve as a barrier in case anyone wanted to do a repeat-McPeake.

It was not outlandish to assume that Heidnik might harbor such thoughts. According to medical records, he was no stranger to suicide attempts. This time, though, there seemed little immediate cause for worry. As he hobbled across the room it was evident he didn't have the strength to sprint the fifteen yards to the windows, even if it had not been for the heavy-duty escort.

When he got to his spot at the defense table, the cuffs were removed and he slid quietly into the straight-backed wooden chair on Peruto's left. He stiffened his spine and sat ramrod straight, just as he had been taught in military school decades before. He stared vacantly at the back wall and outwardly showed little concern with what was going on around him. He might have been in a trance; indeed, he had been diagnosed in the past as catatonic. But as the proceedings progressed, he became more animated. By day two he had dropped his pretense of noninvolvement and was carefully following the action. By day three he had developed a little spring in his step, which was quickly corrected by Peruto. "Shuffle when you walk," he reminded him. "Don't lift your feet." By day four he was laughing and joking with his lawyer.

But he continued to refuse to change his shirt, wash his hair, or bathe. As the days dragged by, Peruto began having second thoughts about the cleverness of his instructions to his client. "When I told him not to shower, I didn't mean forever," Peruto moaned. "A few days of that and he was getting pretty ripe." Eventually, midway through the trial, he begged Judge Abraham to sign a court order forcing Heidnik to take a shower. As his trial moved into its sixth day, Heidnik surprised everyone, even Peruto, by showing up in a rumpled but clean pale-blue, long-sleeved shirt. The next day, though, it was back to the Hawaiian number.

Chapter 33

In sharp contrast to his client's shabbiness, the thirty-three-year-old Peruto was the peacock of Room 653. On the opening day of jury selection he was decked out in a dark suit, burgundy tie on a red-and-white striped shirt with a white collar. His dark beard was trimmed and neatly brushed; his hair was blow-dried and cemented in place. He could have been a model in *GQ*. While waiting for Judge Abraham to appear, he paced nervously around the defense table, occasionally shaking his head. Not a single hair quivered.

On the other side of the narrow aisle was Charles Gallagher, the intent, zipper-lipped prosecutor looking for Heidnik's head on a pike. Since the last time Gallagher was in court on the Heidnik case, he had been promoted from an assistant to a deputy district attorney. If Peruto looked as if he stepped out of a men's fashion magazine, Gallagher wore a slightly rumpled dark suit that looked as though he had dug it out of his seabag a half hour before court and didn't have time to have it properly pressed.

Peruto was flamboyant, a wiseacre, a shoot-from-the-lip lawyer who depended on style as much as substance to make his points with the jury. Gallagher was a plodder, an administrator whose expertise was appellate law. This was his first death-penalty case. He was not in Abraham's courtroom to make a fashion statement or play mind games with jurors. He was there to send a man off to the death house.

Peruto and Gallagher nervously rustled their papers; two fighters dancing in their corners waiting for the bell. Gary Heidnik had been in jail for some four hundred twenty days, and still his trial had not started. They didn't know it yet, but they were going to have to wait a little longer.

If it were up to Peruto, he would wait a *lot* longer. The more successful he could be in delaying the proceedings, the better. If he could postpone the trial another full year, he would be delighted. That would be just that much more time before he faced what all observers considered was the inevitable: Heidnik was almost certainly going to get the stiffest possible sentence. Anything else would be a minor miracle; a victory for Peruto and his client. But the chances of that, he knew, were slim to nonexistent. The momentum had begun. The time of reckoning was at hand.

By all appearances Heidnik was oblivious to this tension. He stared straight ahead, studiously following his lawyer's advice to look disinterested. He may actually *have been* disinterested. The former Army medic, former nurse, self-ordained bishop, church founder, satyr, recluse, and stock market manipulator par excellence, perhaps didn't really seem to *care* if he was shipped off to Rockview and strapped into the electric chair. It may have been some consolation to him, however, to know that although there were about ninety men on death row, Pennsylvania had not executed a criminal since 1962.

The fourth major player in the forthcoming fight,

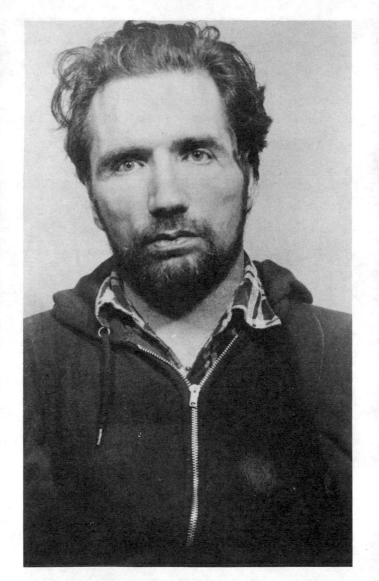

The face of a madman. (AP/Wide World Photos)

Workers remove the body of Deborah Dudley from her shallow grave in New Jersey's forbidding Pine Barrens. (AP/Wide World Photos)

Philadelphia police lead Heidnik from the Sex Crimes Unit soon after his arrest. (AP/Wide World Photos)

Officials from the Philadelphia Medical Examiner's Office remove body parts that were found in Heidnik's refrigerator.
(AP/Wide World Photos)

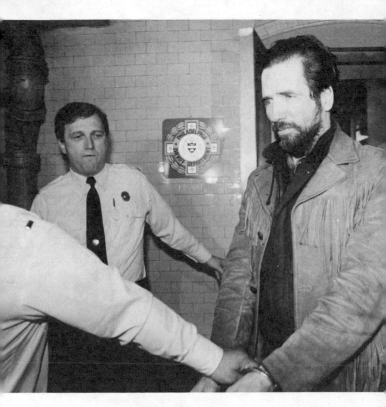

Heidnik is led to court for his preliminary hearing on the murder charges. Incensed inmates in the city jail beat him after his arrest. (AP/Wide World Photos)

A worker removes the section of pipe that was used to shackle Heidnik's victims. (AP/Wide World Photos)

Heidnik, dressed in a festive floral shirt, arrives in court for the first day of his murder trial. (AP/Wide World Photos)

Guilty and condemned to death. (AP/Wide World Photos)

Judge Abraham, looked down through rimless glasses at the mismatched trio before her—the spooky-looking defendant, the dapper defender, and the intense, solemn prosecutor—and struck the gong.

"Let's go into my chambers," she said brusquely.

The invitation did not extend to Heidnik, the press, or the public, only to Gallagher, Peruto, and the court reporter, who silently picked up his stenograph machine and followed the others offstage.

For the next hour Heidnik, a dozen or so spectators, and an almost equal number of reporters were left to their own devices. It was a huge room with a thirty-foot ceiling and a spectator section configured to seat a hundred fifty on straight-backed chairs set up in neat rows. The occupants were so few and the room so large, it seemed virtually empty. But that would change once the trial started; later the room would be jammed with a waiting line outside. On that day, though, Heidnik stared at the wall, alternately clasping his hands in front of him on the table or linking them lightly behind his back. He wasn't asleep, because his legs pumped slowly, methodically. Up. Down. Left. Right. Hour after hour, seldom changing pace; never stopping. Maybe he was nervous. More likely it was because of his medication. Doctors tell people who are taking Stelazine and Thorazine to "pump" their legs before standing to avoid dizziness that comes as a side effect.

Without preamble Peruto and Gallagher reappeared, followed by the court reporter toting his recorder. Abraham swept up the rear and went directly to the bench.

The back-room discussion, she explained, dealt with motions filed by Peruto. His request for a change of venue, that is, to have the trial moved to another city— definitely not "Nome, Alaska," as Peruto had mentioned earlier to reporters as his city of choice—had been withdrawn. He had not, however, given up on his second major petition.

"If I grant Mr. Peruto's request for a change of venire," Abraham said, giving it the Latin pronunciation, *vee-nigh-ray,* "that means the trial will still be held here but the jury will be selected somewhere else."

It was, she added, a motion she was reluctant to grant, at least not without first trying to pick a jury in Philadelphia. The basis for Peruto's request was that Philadelphians had been deluged with too much Garyiana. They had been told so much about the case for so long, Peruto contended, that they could no longer be objective.

The primary question, Abraham declared, was not whether prospective jurors had heard about the case, but whether what they had heard had caused them to form unshakable opinions about Heidnik's guilt.

Before beginning to question jurors, Abraham wanted to get a flavor for what the press, primarily TV, had been saying. With a nod from the judge, a deputy rolled in a dolly supporting a large television set and VCR. Stopping in front of the empty jury box, he swung the equipment so the screen faced Judge Abraham, the two lawyers, and Heidnik. Peruto stepped forward and inserted the first of a series of videotapes into the VCR. As the film reliving Heidnik's arrest and a series of stories that dealt with events that transpired on North Marshall Street was played again and again, a strange thing occurred. Heidnik, who had been studiously ignoring the proceedings up to that point, became more involved. As his image appeared repeatedly on screen—here wearing his favorite leather jacket with the fringes on the sleeves, there being quick-marched into court for a preliminary hearing—he abandoned his aloofness and swiveled his chair to get a better view. His face remained impassive, but his ice-blue eyes darted back and forth as the images flashed in front of him. Occasionally he leaned over and whispered in Peruto's left ear.

When the show was over, Abraham ordered everyone home for the day. On the morrow, she promised, the quest would begin to try to find a dozen unbiased citizens. On Tuesday the first order of business would be the examination of a panel of sixty veniremen.

Chapter 34

May 17-18, 1988

They marched in single file, coming from an anteroom to the judge's right. Abraham had cleared the left side of the spectator section for them, and as they trooped in, they had to travel diagonally across the front of the room, each of them passing within a few feet of Heidnik. As they filed by, each of them gave him a searching glance then quickly looked away. He ignored them, staring unblinkingly at the rear wall. No one had told them what case they might be selected to hear, but by now Heidnik was recognizable to everyone in Philadelphia old enough to watch television, a fact that would be proved within a few minutes.

After they were sworn, en masse, Judge Abraham took over.

This was the case of the Commonwealth versus Gary Heidnik, she explained. No one looked surprised. She paused, examining the group. It was a mixed bag, maybe a few more women than men, but on the whole, pretty evenly matched. They ranged in age from about twenty to about seventy. Roughly half of them were black.

"That's Gary Heidnik," she repeated for emphasis, "not Marty Graham."

Graham's trial ended two weeks earlier in a neighboring courtroom. After waiving a jury, Judge Robert A.

Latrone found him guilty of killing seven women. Minutes after Graham was judged guilty, he was smiling, laughing, and signing autographs for sheriff's deputies. Although the Commonwealth had sought Graham's execution, Latrone, apparently in a moment of compassion, ignored the plea. Instead he handed down a complicated sentence that meant the feebleminded murderer, who at one crucial point in his trial had asked the judge to return his favorite hand puppet—which he called his "Cookie Monster"—would spend the rest of his life in prison.

Latrone sentenced Graham to life for the first murder and death for the other six, plus seven misdemeanor sentences of one to two years each for abusing the corpses of his victims. The way the sentence read, Graham would first serve the misdemeanor sentences then begin the life term. If he ever sought parole on that sentence, the death order would kick in. It was, legal authorities agreed, a very unusual arrangement which was sure to be challenged by the Commonwealth on grounds that death sentences are supposed to take precedence over those specifying life imprisonment. But that was a battle for the higher courts, definitely not something for Judge Abraham to consider. She wasn't, in fact, the least bit worried about Graham or his legal entanglements. She just wanted to make sure the veniremen could separate the two cases in their own minds.

"Would those of you who have heard of the Heidnik case please stand," Abraham commanded. Not surprisingly, everyone did.

For the next twenty minutes she quizzed them as a group, winnowing out the ones who felt Heidnik was guilty and did not think they could change their minds. They would not be acceptable for the jury. Neither would those who were opposed to the death penalty, nor those to whom a month or more of sequestration would pose an undue hardship. When she finished, fifty of the sixty-member panel had been eliminated. But that was only the first round. She sent the remaining ten into an anteroom, from which they would be called individually and questioned further in an attempt to determine their suitability. As soon as they left the room, Peruto jumped to his feet.

"I want to call it to your honor's attention," said Peruto, in a pseudo-outraged tone, "that one of those women was winking at me. She must have winked at me a dozen times."

Abraham smothered a grin. "Which one was it?" she asked sweetly.

"I don't know," Peruto replied, "but she was sitting right there on the front row." Turning, he counted off the number of seats. "Right there," he pointed, "one, two, three, four. The fourth seat from the aisle."

Abraham suggested postponing a decision on the winking woman until she came up for more thorough interrogation. When she did, Peruto dismissed her almost immediately by using one of his precious peremptory challenges.

Under Pennsylvania law, the defense and prosecution each have twenty peremptory challenges—opportunities to dismiss twenty potential jurors without having to offer an excuse. Veniremen also can be disqualified for cause, such as prejudice or extenuating circumstances that would hinder their capabilities as jurors—illness, for example—but that decision has to be made by the judge, usually at the request of the defender or the prosecutor. Peremptory challenges are valuable as each side tries to shape a jury.

At the end of the day four jurors had been selected, a remarkable feat considering the obstacles. Judge Abraham, who still had not ruled on Peruto's motion for a change of venire, was particularly pleased. "I've seen it go slower than this in much-less-publicized cases," she confessed.

But one thing bothered her. All four of the jurors who had been picked were white. During the day, Gallagher had used two of his twenty peremptories and Peruto three. But all three of Peruto's challenges had been against blacks. She was getting the strong impression that Peruto wanted an all-white jury and was going to peremptorily dismiss any black who made it through the initial screening. That, she said, would be intolerable.

Fixing the defense attorney with a hard glare, Abraham warned him that he was tiptoeing through a mine field. "I don't want to have to face accusations that the defense is using discrimination to systematically exclude blacks," she said. "I don't want any charges of reverse discrimination."

Peruto put on his innocent look. "There won't be, your honor," he promised.

Tuesday's feeling of progress carried over into Wednesday.

As on the previous day, all of the sixty veniremen in the panel admitted to having heard about Heidnik and his alleged crimes. But that was hardly unexpected. When the culling was complete, only five potential jurors were left, half as many as the day before. But it was the quality that counted.

During the morning session two jurors were chosen, both white. But Peruto also used two peremptories to dismiss two blacks. After the second one, Judge Abraham straightened and leaned forward, locking her eyes on him. "I'm reserving the right to strike the whole jury," she told him angrily, "if I feel there has been systematic exclusion of blacks."

"I assure you we're not trying to do that," Peruto swore.

At the end of the morning session Abraham had promised to call up another panel in the afternoon. Obviously pleased with the way jury selection was going, she wanted to delay ruling on Peruto's change of venire motion.

Those plans were abruptly cancelled, however, when members of the new panel complained that television crews were filming them in the hallway as they filed into the antechamber preparatory to being examined.

That made her furious. "They're upset, and I don't blame them. They don't want their pictures on TV if they think they're going to be on the jury." Trying to control her temper, she issued a stern warning to the news crews: Either refrain from filming the veniremen, or face orders excluding the cameramen from certain areas of the courthouse.

Before the admonition could be tested, it became moot. Although half a panel had been chosen in only two days, Heidnik insisted, through his attorney, that Abraham approve a change of venire.

Abraham sighed and granted the motion. Three and a half days work went for nothing. Despite numerous requests, it was only the third such entreaty to be granted in Philadelphia in the previous eight years. Abraham set the new voir dire for June 13 in Pittsburgh, three hundred miles away and just about as far west as one can go from Philadelphia and still be in Pennsylvania. On that date she, Peruto, Gallagher, and Heidnik would again begin trying to select an unbiased panel, this time among the residents of Allegheny County.

Chapter 35

Philadelphia's City Hall and the Pittsburgh courthouse both date from the same decade, and both are made from granite. That is all they have in common.

If City Hall looks like a structure from the center of Paris, the Allegheny County Courthouse and Jail, built between 1884 and 1888, resemble buildings that might be found in a medieval countryside; towered and turreted, with faces of rough-cut stone and steeply pitched roofs.

Unlike City Hall, where the interior spaces are littered and dismal, one of the best features of the Pittsburgh facility is its winsome quadrangle, a semi-secluded spot complete with tumbling fountain, leafy trees, comfortable benches, and flowering shrubs. Throughout the day, weather permitting, passersby treat the sun-splashed alcove like a sanctuary, a place to escape the hustle of the city. At noon on Fridays concerts are held there.

But the Philadelphia visitors were not there to sample the cultural amenities. When Judge Abraham and her entourage arrived well past mid-morning, they went straight to Room 315. Judge Robert E. Dauer, the usual occupant, had abandoned the sunny, cheerful chamber and accommodatingly moved into smaller quarters next door so the Philadelphia crew could be more comfortable.

While only about half as large as her usual courtroom back home, Room 315 was much cheerier. It should have put everyone in a happy mood. From the beginning, though, Abraham was out of sorts. Breezing into the building in a dark, pleated skirt and cool-blue silk blouse decorated with large flowers, she was met, not with the anonymity she expected, but chaos. TV lights almost blinded her and still-photographer's strobes winked in her face. "Philadelphia was a [media] freak show," she grumbled. "As soon as I got off the elevator [in Pittsburgh] I saw it was going to be that situation all over again. All we needed was sawdust and peanuts and we would have had a real circus."

It seemed to put her in a bad mood for the entire day. She certainly came down hard on the media. Calling an impromptu news conference, she laid down the law.

"There will be no photos of any prospective jurors or of those who may finally be chosen," she barked. "You will not be permitted to follow them down the street or talk to them. We want an atmosphere of calmness and dignity. I will *not* let you interfere with the trial." Disobedience, she warned, would result in immediate banishment. "I'll keep you out so long your presence here will be totally wasted."

To make her point, she called up a panel of prospective jurors corresponding exactly to the number of available seats: seventy-seven. Since there was, therefore, no room for the press to sit, they would have to go. When Kurt Heine of the *Philadelphia Daily News* asked if she would allow a pool representative to remain, she turned a deaf ear. When the *Inquirer*'s Fen Montaigne protested, she angrily told him to go "file a suit."

When the first prospective juror, a shy middle-aged widow with a cheek full of gum, took the witness stand for detailed quizzing, just about everyone in the room was sizzling. Even though the air conditioner was going full blast and the room was cool enough to serve as a meat locker, steam was rising off just about everyone's brow. Abraham was still fuming at the press, which was mad enough to throw *her* out in the corridor. Peruto was boiling because he didn't like the look of the Pittsburgh panel and the judge had ignored his request to take the whole show on the road once again. On top of that, no one on the panel looked too excited about the prospect of spending half the summer in sticky Philadelphia when they could be in the mountains or on the shore. The only one not grinding his teeth—at least not at that stage— was Gallagher, who remained unruffled despite the turbulence surrounding him.

It turned out to be a short-lived appearance for the nervous widow. Within minutes she was dismissed by Peruto, using the first of his peremptory challenges. Since this was a new proceeding, both he and Gallagher started over again with their allotments. Peruto was now down to nineteen. Looking puzzled but relieved, and still chewing at sixty bites to the minute, the woman hastily exited, only to be followed almost as quickly by a painter for the city school system (a Peruto peremptory), a chubby college coed who begged off because of summer-school classes (dismissed for cause), a half-deaf plumbing inspector (cause), a husky-voiced practical nurse who hesitated when asked about her willingness to impose the death penalty (a Gallagher peremptory), and an eighth-grade dropout who said he thought anyone convicted of first-degree murder should automatically get the chair.

It wasn't until the seventh venireman of the afternoon that both Peruto and Gallagher found a juror they could live with. Somewhat surprisingly, it was an outspoken nurse married to a policeman for twenty-two years. At first this caused Peruto some concern. Tilting back in his chair and stroking his beard with his left hand, he posed a carefully worded question.

"If a police officer were to say something was red and

somebody else said it was blue, would you believe it was red just because a police officer said it?"

"No way," she fired back. "I know police officers too well."

Her response drew laughter from the press, which had finally been allowed inside the courtroom. That prompted another rebuke from Judge Abraham. "We're not here to treat this as a laughing matter," she pointed out.

For a while it looked as though the nurse had stepped over the line as an undesirable juror by admitting that her views could be influenced by her friends and the media. But Abraham led her out of the swamp by eliciting her assurances that she could view the situation with an open mind.

Although eight more prospective jurors were questioned before Abraham knocked off a little after four o'clock, an hour earlier than normal, only two others were selected. One was a taciturn welder with an Elvis haircut who blushingly admitted a brief brush with the law ten years ago when he was fined thirty-seven dollars for starting a barroom ruckus. The other was a well-spoken elementary school teacher's aide—mother of three preteens, and wife to a marketing manager for Westinghouse.

The ones who were *not* selected, however, were as significant as those who were. Among the rejects were a self-possessed young police officer married to a nurse, an indecisive electrical engineer, and two black women—one a data entry clerk and the other a college-educated counselor for a travel agency. Both black women were dismissed by Peruto, who, at the end of the day, had used up seven of his peremptory challenges, one more than one third of his total. And the jury was only one-fourth complete. Gallagher, on the other hand, had used only one peremptory. The others were dismissed by Abraham.

At the rate he was expending his peremptories, things

were not looking up for Peruto. "I want to go back to Philadelphia," he mumbled disgustedly, jabbing forcefully at the down button on the hallway elevator. Despite questioning fifteen prospective jurors, only three had been selected. And this was in a city where the jury pool supposedly had been untainted by media coverage of the case. At the end of the first day the ratio of chosen jurors was well below that of Philadelphia, where four out of seven had been chosen in the opening flurry.

For just about everyone June 13 had turned into a blue Monday. Everyone, that is, except Heidnik. Of all those present, he was the only one who seemed to be enjoying himself. Clad in a different pair of pants but the same old Hawaiian shirt, he perched alertly at the defense table, his slate-blue eyes sparkling and jumping anxiously. While Gallagher plodded through his usual litany of questions in his best Joe Friday drone—just the facts, ma'am, nothing but the facts—Heidnik rocked back and forth in a padded swivel chair that had replaced the wooden straight-back assigned to him in Philadelphia. Twice he laughed aloud, and several times he got into deep, energetic discussions with Peruto. When it came time for him to return to his cell for the night, he even forgot to shuffle.

Chapter 36

June 14, 1988

In Pennsylvania it was Flag Day, a state holiday except in Room 315 of the Allegheny County Courthouse. Judge Lynne Abraham, who was in Pittsburgh to select a jury, not sit around a hotel pool, decreed it would be a working day. It was a spectacularly successful one, as it turned out. In less than four and a half hours, which may have been close to record time, Gallagher and Peruto signed up nine jurors and six alternates, completely filling the panel. Of the original seventy-seven veniremen, two were left when they were through. Even Peruto was happy, which was surprising, considering he'd started off by asking Judge Abraham for another change of venire.

"You have to be joking," she responded when Peruto made his motion. He wasn't, but neither was she. "I can't believe the Supreme Court of Pennsylvania is going to entertain another motion for a change of venire. This is it," she added, ending the discussion.

Despite Peruto's misgivings, the first potential juror called—a frizzy-mopped young hairdresser—was approved in a matter of minutes. That broke the log jam. By lunchtime six more jurors had been picked, including a research chemist who was clearly upset about having to leave his job at Pittsburgh Plate Glass to go to Philadelphia to hear a murder case. His company, he said, would have great difficulty getting along without him. That could be corroborated, he said, by the fact that he had taken only three days vacation at any one time in the last five years.

"PPG is a pretty big company. What would they do if you became ill?" Judge Abraham asked.

"They would not meet their deadlines," the chemist replied.

"That would not be the end of the world," Abraham responded.

The chemist, however, didn't want to give up. He said his absence would result in the loss of "millions of dollars."

Judge Abraham was losing patience.

"That's not money out of your pocket," she said somewhat testily.

"Only so far as I am a stockholder," the chemist shot back.

That was enough for Abraham.

"Inconvenience to your employer is not a hardship. I'm sorry," Abraham said, not looking or sounding sorry at all, "but that's what jury duty is all about."

Gallagher popped to his feet, straightening his coat. "The juror is acceptable to the Commonwealth, your honor."

Abraham cut her eyes to Peruto, who would have the last say on the man's eligibility. "Acceptable to the defense," he blurted, then quickly swiveled so his back was to the bench. His face was as red as a ripe tomato while he struggled to contain his laughter.

The chemist looked as though he were going to cry out in frustration, and finally left the room.

"Boy, was he pissed," Peruto chuckled later. "I just hope he blames it on the prosecution."

A few minutes later another juror, a man married for thirty-seven years, brightened when told he would have to go to Philadelphia to hear the case.

"Can I bring my wife?" he asked innocently, then looked crestfallen when Abraham explained that he would be sequestered and unable to see her.

The final two jurors were selected back to back shortly after the lunch break. When the last member, a sixtyish caseworker for the state Department of Public Welfare, was picked after minimal questioning, Heidnik flashed Peruto a big grin. It was an all-white jury, and Peruto still had half of his peremptories left.

Even with an all-white jury, the panel was impressively diverse. Picked to decide Heidnik's fate were six males and six females ranging in age from their early twenties to their late sixties. The group included one single woman and one divorcée with three grown children, including a son who was a lawyer. There was the hair dresser, a toll collector, a welfare-department caseworker, a derrick-boat operator, the chemist, and a skilled laborer. One man had his own business. One of the jurors was a nurse and another was married to one. Of the six female jurors, all but one worked outside the home at least part time. If there was any common denominator, it appeared to be ancestry. Five had Italian surnames.

A newsman, observing that those of Italian descent might be more conservative and thus inclined to deal more harshly with Heidnik, asked Peruto why he didn't use more of his peremptories to get a more liberal panel.

Peruto was waiting for that one. "They don't know it yet," he quipped, "but my father is president of the Italian Sons and Daughters of America."

With the jury selection out of the way, there was only one thing left to do before opening the trial: haggle over what evidence each side would be permitted to introduce and how far afield they would be allowed to roam in eliciting testimony.

Judge Abraham had already made it clear she planned

to keep a tight reign. Whenever Peruto mentioned that the trial might take three to five weeks, Abraham jumped in. "No way," she said more than once. "This trial is *not* going to take that long. Two to three weeks at most."

To make sure everyone knew the ground rules to which she planned to adhere, Abraham scheduled a hearing in her Philadelphia courtroom on Thursday, June 16, to give Peruto and Gallagher the chance to settle those issues in advance and not tie up valuable trial time.

It had been Peruto's intention to introduce testimony designed to link Heidnik's treatment at the West German military hospital to Army experiments with LSD and other hallucinogens. What he wanted was to create a circumstantial trail showing that Heidnik may have been a guinea pig for drug tests and that the experiments irreparably fried his brain.

The problem was, Judge Abraham wasn't buying it. She wanted to know if Peruto actually planned to pursue this approach.

"Yes, I do," Peruto replied. "If my client were to testify, he would say he went into an Army hospital where LSD experiments had been carried out. He would say he went in for a stomach problem and they gave him something that kept him up for three or four days."

"That's not proof," Abraham said.

"The Army said he would get a one hundred percent disability," Peruto persisted, "but his attorney fought that. He didn't want to leave the Army. He didn't know until published reports in the 1970s that he had been a guinea pig."

Abraham said that all Peruto had offered so far was speculation, and that wasn't going to be enough to allow testimony on the subject.

Proof is hard to come by, Peruto admitted.

"Is it your contention that Mr. Heidnik was one hundred percent mentally well when he went into the Army?" Abraham asked.

"He did have problems," Peruto confessed. "He was psychotic. He wasn't perfect. But that also made him the perfect guinea pig."

"It's a long way from showing he was a perfect guinea-pig subject to being a guinea pig," Abraham commented.

Peruto argued that other things had to be considered as well, such as the Army's desire to get Heidnik out of the service with a full disability. "Only one in eighteen thousand people who file for mental disability get one hundred percent," Peruto said. "And only one in seventy-nine thousand receive it for life. My client gets it for life. And he didn't want it; he didn't file for it."

The judge was unimpressed.

"I haven't heard anything yet about competent evidence that shows me your client was subject to LSD experimentation. You can't use that for mitigation without competent evidence. It would be relevant, but you don't have the evidence," she said.

"If you're asking me if I can put someone on the stand who says my client was given LSD, I can't," said Peruto.

"All you've mentioned so far are conclusions, not proof," said Abraham. "If you have anyone to confirm this, I'll allow it, but from what I've heard so far, you don't."

"It's a clear circumstantial picture," Peruto persisted, unwilling to let go.

"I'm not going to allow any speculation," Abraham repeated. "No guesswork. If you have any competent information about LSD, I'll allow it. But from what you've told me, you're just guessing."

In the end Peruto had to abandon that approach. He didn't have the horses.

There was one more thing Abraham wanted to settle before the trial began: the issue of the all-white jury. Before going to Pittsburgh she vowed that she would not permit an all-white jury to hear the case, but after seeing the racial composition of the Allegheny County venire list, she had softened her stance. "The panel of potential jurors had far fewer blacks than we are used to seeing in Philadelphia," she conceded. "I don't know if [the racial makeup of the jury] is going to be an issue. The tale will be in the telling. In the end, it is not who is on the jury but how it was selected."

She still was not comfortable with the result, she admitted, but she did not plan to strike the entire panel.

"It *is* a racial case," Peruto interjected. "However, please note that I excluded more whites than blacks."

"I'm just noting it," the judge responded. "It may be a nonissue. I'm not taking you to task, I just want you to know that it didn't go unnoticed."

"Any person who puts dog food and human remains in a food processor and calls it a gourmet meal and feeds it to others is out to lunch."

—Peruto

"Just because someone does bizarre acts, the law doesn't recognize them as insane."

—Gallagher

Chapter 37

June 20, 1988

Chuck Peruto considers himself an honest man. He also considers himself a crafty defense lawyer. Not that the two are mutually exclusive, but on opening day he saw an opportunity to be both and he leaped at it.

When he walked into Room 653 in Philadelphia's City Hall, his crisply starched, custom-made shirt already wilting in the blanket of heat and humidity hanging over the city and seeping into the courtroom, he had only an ill-formed plan for his opening statement. But as he sat there listening to Charles Gallagher outline how he intended to prove that Heidnik murdered, raped, kidnapped, assaulted, and did any number of other hideous things to six young women between the ages of eighteen and twenty-five, he had an idea. It was risky, he thought, but it might be worth it. What the hell, he told himself, what does my client have to lose?

Gallagher, looking cool despite the heat, delivered his opening statement in a dull monotone. He didn't have to resort to dramatics to grab the jury's attention. It was the first time the Pittsburghers had heard any specifics about the case, and their eyes popped open. Gallagher was telling them things that went beyond their wildest nightmares. This was horror-movie material. Gallagher didn't have to lay it on.

"Gary Heidnik took these women home with him," Gallagher began. "He plied them with food and in some cases sex. He assaulted them. He choked them. He handcuffed them, and he took them to his basement, where he put muffler clamps on their ankles."

When Gallagher is nervous he fiddles with the flap of his jacket pocket or pulls on his coattail. He displayed both those mannerisms as he paced before the jury.

"He starved them," he continued, his voice steady and matter-of-fact. His left hand dipped briefly into his left jacket pocket. He withdrew it and straightened the flap. "He tortured them. He repeatedly had sex with them." In the process, he added, he killed two of them, one of whose bodies he dismembered, cooked, and fed to the others. Some of the jurors paled. One spectator groaned loudly.

Enough was enough, he thought. He didn't need to overdo it. Once he started calling his witnesses, the testimony would more than speak for itself. But he wasn't quite through. He didn't want to mention the death penalty at this stage, but he did want to get them thinking about first degree. And he felt he had to get them thinking about Heidnik's mental state. He wanted to demolish Peruto's insanity defense before he could make it.

"The evidence will show that from the eve of Thanksgiving 1986 up through March 25, 1987, the defendant committed repeated sadistic and malicious acts," Gallagher said, tugging on the hem of his jacket. "He did them in a methodical and systematic way, and he concealed them in a methodical and systematic way. He knew exactly what he was doing, and he knew it was wrong. He took advantage of underprivileged people."

Gallagher gave a final yank to his coattail and walked back to his chair. His statement took only twelve minutes.

* * *

For several moments Peruto sat motionless—for effect, for theatre.

"You're not required to make an opening statement," Judge Abraham prompted. "You can postpone it until later or you can waive it all together."

"No," said Peruto, springing to his feet. "I want to go ahead." Striding the twenty feet to the jury box, he leaned on the rail, searching for eye contact among the eighteen Allegheny County residents, many of whom still appeared to be in shock by what Gallagher had told them.

"The judge said something this morning about people being innocent until proven guilty," Peruto began, having convinced himself that boldness was the best approach. "My client is not innocent," he said. He paused. "He is very, very guilty." He paused again, a little longer this time.

That was not what he *wanted* to say, he admitted later; it just seemed the *right* thing to say at the time. Before the trial he had offered to plead Heidnik guilty to any charge the district attorney's office wanted except first-degree murder. But there was no compromise in the deputy district attorney's heart; he wanted the death sentence. Peruto was determined he was not going to get it.

Even as he mouthed the words about his client's guilt, he wondered about the wisdom of it. But as he listened to Gallagher he knew he would not be able to refute the charges. He had to be honest, he told himself. His client *was* guilty. He had done everything the Commonwealth said he had. Except for one thing. He had to convince the jury that Heidnik did not intend to kill the two women who died in his cellar. If he could do that, it would not be first-degree murder. Heidnik would dodge the electric chair. The best he could do, Peruto felt, was plant a seed with the jury, give them some reason to start thinking that a man who did everything Heidnik was accused of doing could not possibly be sane. That was his only hope.

"There's no mystery here," Peruto continued. "This is not a whodunit. If all we had to decide here was who did it and what was done, it would be easy."

Gallagher had promised the jury he would construct a trail of evidence leading right to Heidnik's door. Peruto was telling them he didn't want to stop there; he wanted to go one step farther. He intended to open that door and show the man inside.

"You're not here to determine if Gary Heidnik is going to walk out of here a free man," Peruto continued. "He's never going to see the light of day. He will be behind bars or in some mental institution. Any person who puts dog food and human remains in a food processor and calls it a gourmet meal and feeds it to others is out to lunch."

That was inspired, Peruto thought, congratulating himself. Nobody was going to disagree with that, least of all the jurors.

Then he switched direction. He began insinuating that they should consider viewing Heidnik more as a victim and not so much as a cold-blooded killer. When his turn came, Peruto told them, he planned to present overwhelming psychiatric testimony showing that the signs of Heidnik's disintegration had been there for a long time, but no one took the time to read them.

It isn't as though he had never seen a psychiatrist before or never been treated, Peruto said. "He's had twenty-something hospitalizations." Any number of psychiatrists who examined him warned that he was dangerous. Some said he was a time bomb waiting to explode. He was so far gone, Peruto said, that he was no longer able to tell right from wrong.

"You have to keep an open mind," he cautioned, laying the groundwork for his insanity plea. "Dr. McKenzie will testify that Gary Heidnik suffered from such a disease of the mind for so many years that he could not tell right from wrong. Dr. Kool will say the same thing. In fact, you're not going to hear from anybody who came to any other conclusion."

Peruto sensed it was time to quit, time to shut up and sit down. One more point to make. "Understand two things," he said. "One, Gary Heidnik didn't want anybody to die, and two, because of his mental illness, he couldn't tell right from wrong."

His presentation took only nine minutes, three minutes less than Gallagher's.

Not surprisingly, Peruto found he was sweating. So was Gallagher. So was everybody, as a matter of fact. Outside, the thermometer was on its way up to the mid-nineties. Inside, the air-conditioning was broken. It promised to be a long trial.

Chapter 38

It was hard—maybe the hardest thing Jeanette Perkins had ever done. Sitting there in the witness box talking about her dead daughter and staring at her murderer, she wanted badly to cry or scream or jump up and slap his face. But she couldn't. All she could do was answer the questions and pray that he would get what was coming to him. As if he cared. He wouldn't even look at her. Gary Heidnik may as well have been on another planet, from what she could tell. He just sat there staring straight ahead, seeing nothing, saying nothing, maybe hearing nothing too.

Perkins, Gallagher's first witness, tried to ignore Heidnik, tried to forget he was present. Instead she concentrated on the jury, on telling her story to the eighteen men and women sitting a few feet from her on her left and, unlike Heidnik, watching her intently.

A pleasant-looking, middle-aged woman wearing a white dress with blue stripes, Perkins leaned forward slightly to get closer to the microphone. In a calm, soft voice that gave no hint of her inner turmoil, she told the jury that her slightly retarded daughter, Sandra Lindsay, told her on the Saturday after Thanksgiving, 1986, that she was going to the corner store to buy a package of Midol. She never returned.

By Monday, Perkins said, she was starting to get frantic. "It was unusual for her to be gone that long without calling," she explained. First she went to the Elwyn Institute, where her daughter was a client. When she couldn't find her there, she went to the police to report her missing. After that she searched out a man who Sandra had been seeing a lot of: Tony Brown.

Brown had not seen Sandra either, but he suggested Perkins try "Gary's house" at 3520 North Marshall Street. She did. "Me and two of my cousins went there and knocked on the door. We could hear the music playing real loud, but nobody answered our knocks. We went back at seven-thirty, but nobody came to the door then either."

A week to the day after Sandra disappeared, Perkins said, she received a note in her daughter's hand. It was mailed the previous day from New York. A few days afterwards she received a Christmas card from Sandra, also postmarked New York.

Despite the correspondence, she could not shake the feeling that it was all a hoax; it was too much out of character for her daughter. Another daughter and the cousins made several more trips to the North Marshall Street address, but no one ever came to the door. The next thing she knew, she said, police were knocking on *her* door to tell her that parts of a body found in a freezer at 3520 North Marshall Street were believed to be Sandra's.

Peruto did not cross-examine. But when Perkins was cornered by reporters in the hallway, she said that the police should have done more. That time when she spoke, the tears started flowing.

Peruto may have been kind to Perkins by waiving his chance to question her, but he had no reason to be gentle with Gallagher's second witness, police sergeant Julius

Armstrong, the slim, black officer who handled Perkins' missing-person report.

During direct examination Armstrong, a veteran of seventeen years with the department, explained that he, too, had gone to the North Marshall Street house. He got no response to his knocks, either, and no one answered the phone when he called. He also looked up Tony Brown and got Gary's last name from him. Brown misspelled it, but Armstrong admitted he did not double check. When he fed the name Brown gave him into the police computer, it came up blank. Then, when Perkins told him about the note and the card, he rested much easier. From then on, he confessed, he did not give the search a lot of thought.

"You knew [Gary's] name and you knew the address?" Peruto asked.

"Yes," replied Armstrong.

"Did you ever check the tax rolls or the utility files to see what Gary's last name was?"

"No."

"Tony Brown is a little slow, isn't he?"

"He seemed all right to me."

"Did you go next door and ask the people if they had seen Sandra?"

"No," Armstrong said, then quickly added, "I was satisfied she was safe when we got the letter from New York."

Peruto gave him a disgusted look and slumped in his chair. "No more questions."

Gallagher's third witness was his star: Josefina Rivera.

She walked quickly and proudly to the stand, her head held high. Taking the oath with her hand on the Bible, she looked straight at Heidnik. He glanced at her quickly, then ignored her just as he had Perkins and Armstrong. Just, in fact, as he would almost everyone called to testify.

Of the four surviving captives, Rivera would be the most articulate. In a low-pitched, sedate voice, the thin former prostitute, wearing a stylish sun dress decorated with large blue flowers and a huge, flowing wig, described her capture, her imprisonment, and the indignities she was forced to endure.

The courtroom was packed, but there was no chatter, no comment. At the more gruesome parts of the testimony some of the spectators moaned softly, but Judge Abraham had sternly warned the audience about displays. "If anyone interrupts, they will be arrested and jailed," she pronounced. "I won't permit any outbursts, no matter how sad or bizarre the testimony is."

On the first day she was a captive, Rivera said, she listened in fascination as Heidnik told her how he planned to bring other women into the cellar, impregnate them and start a colony.

"Why did he say he wanted to do this?" Gallagher asked innocently. It was, in fact, a loaded question. He knew, although the jury did not, that her answer would open a door revealing Heidnik's criminal record. If he had not been able to introduce the issue through Rivera, he may not have been able to bring it up at all because it would, by its very nature, be prejudicial to Heidnik. The fact that he planned to do this was brought out in discussions out of the jury's presence earlier in the day. Peruto opposed it vigorously, but Judge Abraham agreed to allow it if Gallagher could introduce it through Rivera. It was the first of Abraham's rulings that seemed to come down heavily on the side of the prosecution. It would not be the last.

Rivera testified that Heidnik was obsessed with having children because he had been sent to prison for trying to help the sister of the woman he had been living with. The woman, Anjeanette Davidson, had a daughter by him. The girl had been placed in a foster home.

"He said he went away for five years, and when he

came out he couldn't find Anjeanette and he felt he had been deprived of his family. He felt as though society owed him a wife and family."

Several of the jurors looked surprised when Heidnik's prison record was revealed. Abraham interrupted: "Don't try to interpret that," she told the jury, letting the statement hang. Later, from other witnesses, they would hear a lot more about the crime and Heidnik's prison record.

Without skipping a beat, Rivera continued her tale. She told how the others—Sandra Lindsay, Lisa Thomas, Deborah Dudley, Jacquelyn Askins, and Agnes Adams— were brought in one by one, and about how they, too, were abused and misused.

"What did he feed you?"

Rivera shrugged. "Crackers . . . oatmeal . . . rice . . . hot dogs . . . sometimes waffles . . . chicken . . . bread . . . water . . . hot chocolate. Usually we would eat early in the morning and late at night."

Did he say anything about Lindsay having his baby?

"He said Sandra had promised to have a baby by him, but she kept backing out, and this time she wouldn't be able to."

"What did you do to pass the time?" Gallagher wanted to know.

"Nothing too much," she replied nonchalantly, "outside of just having sex and staying in the hole. Three times we were down in the hole and we ran out of air and we couldn't breathe. We started screaming and hollering, and Gary came down and beat us . . . We didn't take any baths or wash our hair. We just had baby washcloths . . . Music was going twenty-four hours a day."

The hygiene situation improved after Christmas, she added. "Then everybody had a day to go bathe. He would take your chains off the sewer pipe and take you upstairs and put you in the tub with the chains, and afterwards he would take you in a little bedroom and have sex with you."

By the end of January, when there were five captives, they were actively considering plans to overpower Heidnik and escape, said Rivera. "We had an escape planned for January twenty-ninth but nothing was done. Gary had heard us talking about it."

Chapter 39

For more than three hours Josefina Rivera buried Gary Heidnik with a wealth of detail, mainly about the deaths of Sandra Lindsay and Deborah Dudley.

"He had Sandra on bread and water and he kept her chained with one arm over her head. She had been throwing up and she said she wasn't feeling good. She passed out once . . . [and] I asked Lisa to go over and make her stand up. She stood up for twenty or thirty minutes, but then she collapsed . . . Gary came down and undid her handcuff, and her body just crashed to the floor . . . then he kicked her into the hole and got in there with her and said she was dead."

"What happened after that?" Gallagher prompted.

"He carried her upstairs and we heard an electric saw, and then we smelled a terrible odor. He smelled like it and so did the food he brought us."

"Did he have sex with anyone that night?"

"No."

"How about the next day?"

"Yes, with Lisa and [Askins]."

Rivera said Heidnik had stopped beating her early in January, apparently because he was beginning to feel he could trust her. Besides, she said, he was having continuing problems with Dudley, and that occupied much of his time.

"He always had trouble with Debbie . . . Debbie always fought back."

Not long after Lindsay died, Heidnik took Dudley upstairs on a mysterious mission.

"In about five minutes she came back," Rivera said. "She was very quiet."

Finally Dudley told the others what had occurred. Rivera remembered her saying, "He showed me Sandra's head cooking in a pot, and her ribs were cooking in a roasting pan in the stove, and her legs and arms were in the freezer." He told Dudley that if she kept it up, it would happen to her. Six weeks later Dudley, too, was dead.

"Everybody went on punishment in early March," Rivera said. "We were eating dog food mixed with body parts." Over a period of days, the punishment became more severe. Finally, Rivera said, Heidnik filled the hole with water, put Thomas, Askins, and Dudley inside, and began shocking the three with a bare electric cord which he placed in contact with Dudley's chain. When she collapsed, Heidnik thought she was faking. "He said, 'She can't be dead.' Then he went over and looked at her and said, 'She's dead.' "

After that, Rivera testified, Heidnik began trusting her because he made her sign a letter saying she was responsible for Dudley's death.

On March 24, after promising to find him another woman, Rivera was able to get away alone. She went to the cops.

"Until then," Gallagher asked, "did you have any chance to escape?"

"No."

"What did he say would happen?"

"He said he would kill the other girls."

* * *

Although it was late in the afternoon, Peruto was anxious to begin his cross-examination. If he could shake Rivera, he felt, he could perhaps insert that seed of doubt in the jurors' minds. At the preliminary hearing in the spring of 1987 he had attempted to prove that Rivera played a much larger role in what happened to the other women than she had admitted. He was going to have a second chance to see if he could get her to crack.

"Why did he say he was keeping you captive?" Peruto asked.

"He wanted us to have children," Rivera answered. Her tone had changed from that used with Gallagher. Her voice was still impersonal, but now it carried a heavy overlay of hostility.

"Why did he pick the cellar?"

"He said he didn't want to do it in the conventional way because the city kept taking them away."

Peruto was trying to make a point; he wanted to show how unbalanced Heidnik was. "How many women did he say he wanted and how many babies?"

"He wanted ten women to have ten children, all in the basement."

"He walked, talked, and acted the same, but what he was doing may not be what you would do, right?"

"Yes."

Peruto let a long silence build while he and Rivera glared at each other.

"Before you went to the police, you went to your boyfriend, is that right?"

"Yes."

"What did you tell him?"

"I told him I had been held captive for four months."

"Was there anything else to it?"

"No."

"Your boyfriend is your pimp, isn't he?"

"No," Rivera answered angrily. "I never worked for anybody but myself."

"Are you aware you're being sued by the other victims because of your connection with Heidnik?"

"No."

"Are you wearing a wig today?"

This flustered Rivera. "Yes," she stammered.

Try as he might, Peruto was unable to make much headway. At one point he tried to get her to confess that she and her boyfriend, Vincent Nelson, planned to rob Heidnik before calling the police. She denied it.

"Did you get any of your information from the media?" Peruto asked, trying to show she used news reports to embellish her tale.

"I was there," she shot back. "I don't need to get it from the newspapers."

Although he was able to get her to admit that there were times when Heidnik was not supervising her and she could have escaped, she said if she had, he simply would have taken it out on the others. Her plan all along, she said, was to work her way into Heidnik's trust and bide her time until she could assure the safety of the others as well as herself.

Peruto sat silent, looking for a new line of attack.

"Is it a fair statement that you would like to see the defendant convicted of first-degree murder?" he asked.

Rivera shot a venomous glance at Heidnik. "That's right," she spat.

Judge Abraham called time. It had been a long day, she said, and the temperature in the courtroom was nearing the boiling point. Peruto could resume his cross-examination on Tuesday. It would give everyone a chance to cool off.

Chapter 40

June 21, 1988

The cool-down period didn't take: not for the weather, not for the participants. It was even hotter in the courtroom on Tuesday than it had been the previous day, so hot, in fact, that the first thing Judge Abraham did was take off her robe and invite the lawyers to remove their jackets. Peruto did; Gallagher didn't. The jurors had anticipated this development. When they appeared, most of the men had abandoned their ties for golf shirts and the women gave up their suits for sun dresses. It was time to get down to business.

The battle between Peruto and Rivera was no less bitter on Tuesday, but it *was* much shorter. Rivera had swapped her dress for a white blouse and purple slacks and her big wig for a less ostentatious one. It was the only indication that Peruto had gotten to her at all. She had not left any of her hostility toward the defense at home.

Again Peruto was unable to get her to admit complicity or to trap her into contradicting her testimony at the 1987 hearing. After about ten minutes he gave up and turned her back over to Gallagher for redirect.

The DDA had three more points he wanted to make before he let her go, three more things to show that

Heidnik knew what he was doing during the period he held the women hostage.

· He asked Rivera what was the first thing Heidnik did when they drove back into Philadelphia after dumping Dudley's body in New Jersey.

"He stopped to buy an *Inquirer* so he could check his stocks," Rivera said.

· He asked why Heidnik had stopped to get another woman to go with them when they went to pick up Heidnik's Rolls at the garage, and why he took that woman home with them to play video games.

"She was Sandy's friend," Rivera said, "and he wanted her to see inside the house so she could go to [Lindsay's] family and tell them she wasn't there."

· Gallagher asked Rivera if she knew where Heidnik got his ideas.

"Yes," she answered brightly. "He got them from watching movies and TV. He got the idea for feeding us parts of Sandy's body from the movie *Eating Raoul,* and his ideas on punishment from *Mutiny on the Bounty.* He also saw [*The World of*] *Susie Wong,* and he liked the way Oriental women were. That's why he picked a Filipino wife."

Gallagher called two more witnesses: one of the policemen who arrested Heidnik, and an attractive black policewoman who questioned Rivera. The latter testified to Rivera's condition when she was first brought in— "she was trembling, crying," said Officer Denise Turpin.

With the groundwork laid, Gallagher called the other three captives in quick succession.

Lisa Thomas, now a chunky twenty-year-old with her hair in braids, took the stand wearing turquoise slacks, a T-shirt, and long, dangly earrings.

For the most part the story of her capture paralleled Rivera's, as did those of Jacquelyn Askins and Agnes Adams. But the details were no less horrific.

The day after attaching her shackles and leaving her to join Rivera and Lindsay, Heidnik seemed to experience a touch of compassion and substituted a longer chain for the one connecting her ankles.

"Why did he do that?" Gallagher asked.

"So I could open my legs wider to have sex," she said.

"Did he beat you too?" the DDA inquired.

"Yes," she said. "Almost from the first moment. I said something to make him mad, and he said he was going to hit me. He did. He hit me five times with a thick, brown stick."

"Was there anything else?"

"He told me to beat Sandy regularly; he'd get his kicks from seeing us beat each other . . . He'd get on top of me and make me suck his penis. He said if I didn't, he would beat me."

On cross-examination Thomas at first said she couldn't remember her earlier testimony about Rivera beating the others even when Heidnik wasn't there.

"Oh, yeah, I remember," she said. "Nicole [Rivera] would laugh when she put water in the hole [prior to electric-shock torture]. The electric shocks were her idea."

"[Rivera] was just feeding a sick mind, wasn't she?" Peruto asked quickly, seeing an opening.

"Objection," Gallagher screamed, jumping to his feet.

"Sustained," Judge Abraham said quickly, giving Peruto a withering look.

"What else would she do?" Peruto continued.

"She and Gary would go out and then they would come back and brag about what they had done that day."

"Did you ever plan an escape?"

"Yeah, but then Nicole told Gary about it."

Gallagher regained some of the lost ground on redirect, getting Thomas to clarify that Rivera was always in chains until Dudley was electrocuted. While Peruto made much more headway with Thomas than he had with Rivera, his path was unclear. Was he defending Heidnik or prosecuting Rivera?

Jacquelyn Askins looked scared to death. The youngest of the captives, she was still only nineteen when she took the stand. Her eyes, which had a slight Oriental tilt, were brimming with tears and her voice shook. She was hooking on a street corner at lunchtime when Heidnik picked her up, took her home, had sex with her, handcuffed her and took her to the cellar. The first thing he did to her in the basement was whip her with a switch. That night, she added, he decided to have a "party." Her description of the events was the first (and last) testimony to indicate Heidnik indulged in group sex.

"I'd suck his penis and another girl would suck his balls," she said. "Then he'd have sex with one girl and I'd lie next to him so I could catch his juice."

Later Heidnik seemed concerned about Askins getting enough to eat. She was so petite that the muffler clamps Heidnik used on the other women were too large for Askins' ankles. He had to use handcuffs. When it seemed as though she was not eating properly, he brought her instant breakfasts and peanut butter-and-jelly sandwiches —rare treats in Heidnik's cellar.

"Debbie was so hungry she said she'd eat dog food," Askins said. "After that, we all got dog food."

She said Heidnik was constantly testing them, pushing them to see how they would react, perhaps to give him another excuse to beat them. Even when police rushed in to rescue them, Askins was not sure it was not another Heidnik ruse. "I thought [the police raid] was him," said Jacquelyn Askins. "I thought he was trying to get us to scream so he could beat us."

The petite teenager was coming apart on the stand, quietly sobbing and dabbing at her eyes with a wadded handkerchief. Peruto studied her quietly for a few seconds and decided to waive cross-examination.

As Askins left the room on the arm of a burly matron from the district attorney's office, those inside the courtroom were jolted by a loud piercing scream and a husky voice yelling, "Get away, get away." Askins had been waylaid by the camera crews waiting in the hallway.

Judge Abraham's face turned red. "Bring them all in here," she ordered. "Right now."

With the jury out of the room, Abraham angrily lectured the half-dozen photographers and cameramen lined up before the bench.

"You don't have any sympathy at all," she told them. "If that were your mother or sister, you'd be the first to punch someone out. That was a cheap, tawdry trick to play on a victim, and you ought to be ashamed. You have no sensitivity, no feeling, no sense of dignity. You have nothing going for you except your cameras."

She took the one course of punishment open to her: she ordered them away from the courtroom. "You're off the floor," she said furiously. "I'll have the sheriff remove you. You're out. If you want to take pictures, you're going to have to do it from outside."

Dismissing them, she stalked into her chambers to cool off. As she did, the spectators in the jammed courtroom applauded loudly. It was a demonstration she did not try to control.

Twenty minutes later testimony resumed when Gallagher called the last captive, Agnes Adams, to the stand.

Adams' tale differed from the others by the fact that she had been with Heidnik twice before the night he took her captive. She met him the first time, she said, around the end of 1986 or early 1987, when he picked her off a street corner and offered her money for sex. They went to the North Marshall Street house but couldn't get in the driveway because a car had it blocked. Neither could Heidnik find a parking place, so he paid her for her time and dropped her off.

The second time was March 20, 1987. That time, he took her to his bedroom and had sex with her. Afterwards, he let her out the back door. He carefully locked it behind her. The third time, she said, was on the night of March 23, when she was approached by Heidnik and Rivera together. She said she also knew Rivera—although she was then using the alias Vanessa—from the days when they both worked in the same strip club.

She said she left with them in Heidnik's Cadillac, went to North Marshall Street, and had sex with Heidnik while Rivera waited in the living room downstairs. It was then that Heidnik handcuffed her and dragged her into the basement.

During cross-examination Peruto got her to concede that Rivera could have left Heidnik's house at any time while she and Heidnik were upstairs. She also said she had seen Rivera at a northside street corner two weeks before she was captured, which would have been more than a week before Rivera claimed she was released from chains. Afterwards Peruto admitted that Adams had been mistaken about the sighting.

In only two days the Commonwealth had presented its major witnesses—a process that Gallagher originally estimated would take at least twice as long. Proceedings were moving much faster than everyone had expected. If all went well, Gallagher promised Judge Abraham, he would finish his case-in-chief by lunchtime on Wednesday. He proved to be right on target.

Chapter 41

June 22, 1988

Before Charles Gallagher could rest his case, however, there were still some loose ends to be tied up. With the jury out of the room, Gallagher, Peruto, and Judge Abraham waded through a large pile of exhibits the Commonwealth wanted to enter as evidence. Gallagher was relentless about exhibits. Before the trial was over he had offered almost two hundred items ranging from photographs of the site where Dudley's body was found to a red plastic bucket full of chains. The DDA also proffered a series of slides showing the body parts found in Heidnik's freezer, but Abraham previewed them in her chambers and decided the jury didn't need them. By the time they finished sorting through the items and the jury was summoned, it was well after mid-morning.

When the court recessed on Tuesday, police lieutenant James Hansen was on the stand. A veteran homicide detective, Hansen had been in charge of the search party at Heidnik's house and had later headed the investigation. Most of his testimony dealt with the physical evidence Gallagher wanted to introduce.

Hansen, however, did add one piece to the growing puzzle. Peruto managed to get from him the fact that there was a second person—Cyril "Tony" Brown—charged in connection with the events in Heidnik's cellar.

The jurors looked puzzled when Brown's name came up, and Judge Abraham quickly ordered the defense attorney to abandon that line of questioning.

"You can't ask any questions about him," Abraham ruled abruptly.

The rest of Gallagher's witnesses were scene setters. A detective who headed the search for Deborah Dudley's body testified in excruciating detail about the route he and Rivera followed as she tried to lead him to the site. Dr. Robert Catherman, the deputy medical examiner who performed the autopsy on Dudley, confirmed she had died of electrocution. "It was an almost classic example of electrothermal injury," he said dispassionately.

Catherman also mentioned one other curious fact: Dudley's body showed clear evidence of recent considerable weight loss. "She had a lot of excess skin," he said. "She had more skin than body." That condition occurs, he added, when there is rapid weight loss and the skin has not had time to shrink to adjust to the loss of fat.

Other witnesses came and went quickly. There was Dudley's sister, Diane Dudley, a handsome woman with close-cropped hair, who told the jury the last time she had seen Deborah was on Thanksgiving, six weeks before she disappeared.

Officer Julio Aponte testified that he responded to neighbors' complaints about a terrible smell on North Marshall Street in February 1987 but did not investigate further after Heidnik told him he had simply burned his dinner.

"You realize you don't burn your dinner for days, don't you?" Peruto asked on cross-examination.

"I don't know that," Aponte replied. "I don't cook."

"Didn't you tell us that you actually observed something cooking in the pot on the stove?"

"Yes."

"Did you ask [Heidnik] about that pot?"

"No."

"Did you ever smell anything like that in your life?"

"No."

"So you were satisfied that everything was all right?"

"I had no reason to believe anything was wrong. He was alive."

Another grisly bit of testimony came from Dr. Paul Hoyer, the assistant medical examiner who studied the parts taken from Heidnik's freezer.

In addition to the frozen parts, Hoyer said, investigators found in the yard fragments of a bone from an upper left arm that were the same size and shape as a matching body part found in the freezer. "The fragments had dog hairs on it," Hoyer said.

In the oven there were several rib fragments, a number of tooth fragments, and one whole tooth. "The intact tooth had a very unusual wear pattern," Hoyer testified. "But when we looked at a photograph [of Sandra Lindsay], we saw that she had a very unusual bite pattern." Investigators also found in the stove several hand fragments, skull fragments, part of a shoulder bone, and a piece of vertebra. "There was nothing there to suggest the remains were from more than one individual," he added.

Hoyer said identification was made by studying a left wrist that was found in the freezer. Lindsay had injured her wrist a year before and an X ray was on file. That was compared with the wrist found in the freezer. "The overall shape and size matched," said Hoyer, "plus the pattern matched. There is a pattern in bone, and each pattern is unique. By comparing this we were able to say this was Sandra Lindsay."

From the parts remaining, however, he said he had been unable to determine how Lindsay died. "But I can say her death was unnatural, based on the extreme effort to which someone went to conceal the death. We ruled that the manner of death was homicide."

Peruto asked Judge Abraham to strike Hoyer's testimony regarding the homicide conclusion.

"Nope," Abraham answered.

"I move to strike the cause of death," Peruto persisted.

Again Abraham refused. "I don't think the method of death needs to be proved to determine murder," she said. "The question is, has the Commonwealth established this was an unlawful killing?"

Gallagher rose and straightened his pocket flap. "The prosecution rests," he said.

Immediately Peruto was on his feet asking Judge Abraham to remove the charge of first-degree murder. "There was no specific intent to kill," he argued.

"Overruled," Abraham said.

Glancing at the clock over the door, she ordered a recess. The defense would begin its case after lunch.

Chapter 42

Chuck Peruto could hardly have gotten off to a worse start.

His first witness was Dr. Clancy McKenzie, a plumpish, frizzy-haired, unconventional psychiatrist who looked as much like a shrink as Santa Claus looks like an IBM executive. With his blue suspenders and detached grin, McKenzie had a folksy, relaxed air about him. When he spoke, it was slowly, deliberately, almost shyly. Jurors sized him up quickly and were prepared to like him. They could even be ready to listen to him.

There was a problem, though. Judge Abraham had no use for him.

Ironically, McKenzie almost didn't squeak through the prosecution challenge of his credentials to qualify as an expert witness.

With his own psychiatric witness, the much sought-after Dr. Robert Sadoff, hanging over his shoulder and feeding him questions, Charles Gallagher put McKenzie through the paces.

"Do you belong to the American Psychiatric Association?"

"I did, but I dropped my membership."

"How long ago?"

"About three years ago."

"Do you belong to any professional institutions or organizations?"

"No, I do not."

"Do you have any publications?"

"Some. I have written about my work."

"Any specific publications?"

"No."

"You have not written?"

"No, that's not true. I didn't send my work in for publication."

"How much work have you done in forensic psychiatry?"

"I've testified maybe half a dozen times. It's not what I choose to do."

"How many criminal cases?"

"Two."

With a smirk, Gallagher sat down. If he had chosen to object to McKenzie's qualification, he might well have been backed by Judge Abraham. On the other hand, if he did not object, McKenzie might damage Peruto's case more than help it—at least that's what Gallagher seemed to be banking on.

While Gary Heidnik had shown little interest in the testimony of any of the witnesses called so far, he listened intently as McKenzie spoke. Since shortly after his arrest until the trial started, Heidnik and McKenzie had met thirty times for a total of almost one hundred hours. That was infinitely more time than Heidnik spent with all of the other psychiatric witnesses combined. Obviously he and McKenzie got along.

If McKenzie could have stuck to what was asked him, his testimony might have been a major benefit for the defense. As it was, it turned into a distinct liability.

"I can't understand it," Peruto complained later. "During our prep sessions he was right on target; he had everything together. Then when he got on the stand, he just refused to take any direction. He had his own agenda; he wanted to present *his* theory and he wouldn't take my guidance at all."

Indeed, from the beginning McKenzie exhibited a tendency to say what *he* wanted to say rather than what Peruto wanted him to say. Heidnik's defense would have been better served, by far, if the psychiatrist would have let the lawyer be the quarterback.

"I'm not here so much to defend Gary Heidnik as to explain him," McKenzie began. "I believe you should never judge a man until you've walked in his moccasins, and it's pretty hard to walk in Gary Heidnik's moccasins."

It was his theory, he said, that every schizophrenic has two minds—that of the adult and that of the troubled infant—in one skull.

"Is Gary Heidnik schizophrenic?" Peruto asked.

"Oh, yes," McKenzie replied.

"Between November 1986 and April 1987 did he know right from wrong?"

"During that four to five month period he could not have known right from wrong. But what I'm going to talk about are events that occurred twenty years ago—"

"If you're going to start back in history," Judge Abraham interrupted, "you're going to lose the jury long before you get to where you want to go."

"What caused his schizophrenia?" Peruto queried.

"Ah," said McKenzie. "This is my forte. There is a survival mechanism in everyone. If you give a puppy a powerful electrical shock and then, as grown dogs, they are shocked again, they retreat to puppy behavior . . ."

"I don't want to give the jury a medical degree," said Peruto, losing patience. "Listen to me very carefully. Specifically, what finding did you come to regarding Gary Heidnik?"

"In schizophrenia every piece of behavior matches the behavior of an infant . . . everything the mentally disturbed person experiences relates in some way to infancy. The most common thing I've found was the birth of a brother or sister in the first eighteen months of life. Gary Heidnik had a brother seventeen months younger—"

Judge Abraham broke in and tried to bring McKenzie back on track. "You're killing them with words, Doc." Her effort was unsuccessful. He ignored her.

"Trauma in the present returns an adult to trauma in the past," McKenzie continued. "I explored every one of Gary Heidnik's acts to see if it came from a seventeen-month-old brain or if it came from an adult brain. If it came from the seventeen-month-old brain, Gary Heidnik wouldn't be able to tell right from wrong—"

"Just answer everything in one or two words," Peruto interjected. "If it requires elaboration, no more than fifteen. What trauma did Gary Heidnik have when he was seventeen months old?"

McKenzie didn't answer. Instead he launched into a long, complicated explanation of schizophrenia.

"The jury is never asked to define schizophrenia, just to determine if he knew right from wrong," said Abraham. "The jury doesn't have to know what all the ramifications are."

"He had a sibling born when he was seventeen months old," McKenzie said. "His wife left him the first time, and he tried to commit suicide. Then she came back and left him again in April 1986, and that started the whole thing. He decided no woman was ever going to leave him again and no one was going to take his babies away again. This was the fourth time. He went totally berserk. He gets the women, chains them up, then develops this concept that he's going to raise normal babies in his basement. That's the seventeen-month-old brain."

"Why did he like retarded women?" Peruto asked.

"He felt rejected, so he sought those who were also rejected."

Peruto asked how this fit in with his treatment of the women in the cellar.

"Like a baby would do with a pet," said McKenzie. "Shove a couple of pieces of bread in its mouth. When he had to dispose of the bodies, it was like a two-year-old trying to hide the candy wrappers. He put body parts in a pot on the stove, in the oven, in the backyard, everywhere. The only thing he didn't do was run them up the flagpole. Do you know why he put body parts in the freezer? He was planning to start the babies—once they were off the breast—on human flesh. Infants suck for six months, and then they have a wish to devour the mother's flesh. This was the infant brain beyond a shadow of a doubt . . . He punished the way he was punished as a child . . . He had a beer party for them every Friday night. He had hot buttered popcorn. When he heard the girls were planning to kill him, the punishment got worse . . . one day some dog food dropped on the floor and one of the girls came along and scooped it up. He couldn't understand why anyone would want to eat dog food—"

"How could he make stock investments?" Peruto interjected.

"At the time he became very ill he made very poor investments . . . He lost a hundred thousand dollars in a very short time when he started getting ill . . ."

At two minutes before four o'clock, a half hour before the normal quitting time, a frustrated and exhausted Peruto turned McKenzie over to Gallagher for cross-examination. You could almost hear the DDA licking his chops.

Chapter 43

Charles Gallagher, cross-examiner, was not the same as Charles Gallagher, prosecutor. So far in the trial, Gallagher had been quiet, noticeably polite, restrained, almost deferential. As a cross-examiner he became arrogant, loud, and impatient. It was a new persona, and he picked a good time to reveal it: Clancy McKenzie was still on the stand. Before he could begin really grilling the psychiatrist, though, there were some other matters to be dealt with.

With the jurors not yet in their seats, Peruto told Judge Abraham that he was considering asking that the judge instruct the jury to consider the possibility that Josefina Rivera was an accomplice to Gary Heidnik.

"If the defendant is clever enough to enlist the aid of an accomplice, he knows what he's doing," Abraham said. "This could be a problem if you charge Rivera. . . . If you want an accomplice charge, I'll give you one, but Rivera is no fool. It is no great leap to say if your client got someone to work with him, if he's smart enough to get an accomplice, he's not insane. Why don't you talk it over with your client."

In the courtroom it was hotter than ever. The day before in Philadelphia, for the first time in eleven years, the temperature had hit a hundred degrees. When the jurors filed in, only two of them wore jackets. Peruto hung his over the back of his chair, but Gallagher kept his on. Giving his coattail a quick jerk, the DDA opened up on McKenzie with evident relish.

"What is the legal definition of insanity?" Gallagher asked, trying to determine if McKenzie knew the provisions of the "M'Naghten Rule." Adopted in England in 1843 and later imported to this country, M'Naghten (named after an insane Scots woodcutter who tried to assassinate the prime minister) holds that a person shall not be held responsible for criminal acts if he, because of a "disease of the mind," is unable to know the "nature and quality" of his acts, or does not know that such acts are wrong. It is a standard used in courtrooms in twenty-five states besides Pennsylvania.

"A person did not know . . ." McKenzie began, then fumbled for words. "I don't have the textbook definition."

Gallagher handed him a photocopy of a page from the Pennsylvania statues. McKenzie read: ". . . someone who did not know what he was doing or did not know right from wrong."

"Which is it?" Gallagher demanded.

"Both."

"Did he know what he was doing between November and April?"

"I'd have to go to my diagram . . ."

"Did he pick up a mentally deficient woman to satisfy his sexual desire?"

"I don't agree with that statement."

"Did he know when he lured mentally deficient girls to his basement?"

"No. But which 'he' are you speaking of? His adult brain or his infant brain?"

"Did the adult brain know?"

"The adult brain was operating in greatly diminished capacity."

"Yes or no?"

"The adult brain had only partial awareness. It knew what he was doing when he was driving a car, but it was not there sufficiently . . . No, absolutely he did not know right from wrong."

"Did Heidnik know it was wrong when he proceeded to conceal the identity of Sandra Lindsay by dismembering her and destroying the head and fingerprints?"

"No. There was not enough adult mind present . . . it was not until he was thrown into jail and someone beat him up and he was given anti-psychotic medicine that he came out of it. When he was shown their pictures he didn't even recognize them, except for Sandra, who was a good friend of his. That's because he was looking at them with his infant brain. His adult brain hadn't seen them."

"Is there a possibility he was faking it?"

"Absolutely not."

"Is it possible he was . . . telling you lies to get an advantage over you?"

"Absolutely not."

"Isn't it true that someone can fake mental illness?"

"He can't fake schizophrenia with *me,*" McKenzie insisted.

McKenzie was excused soon afterwards, much to Peruto's relief. Gallagher gave a small grin. He rather enjoyed it.

At this point in the trial a strange thing became noticeable: Judge Abraham also appeared to assume a new persona, one that certainly appeared pro-prosecution. Given her background as a highly aggressive prosecutor, it would not have been unusual for her sympathies to be in that camp. Also, she might have been having great difficulty remaining unbiased toward Gary Heidnik, considering the viciousness of his acts. But, discernably, her temper was getting shorter with Peruto. Their personalities might have clashed under the best of conditions, and the tensions within a courtroom were not conducive to improving relations.

Whatever it was, it began emerging when Clancy Mc-Kenzie was on the stand and grew steadily more pronounced. Clearly, she had little patience with the psychiatrist, and at times was overtly scornful. There was, as well, another incident relating indirectly to McKenzie.

One of the first actions Abraham took after being assigned the case was to issue a gag order prohibiting the lawyers from talking to the media. Ostensibly, it was an attempt to keep publicity in check until a jury could be selected. But the order continued in force even after the jury was picked and sequestered. The lawyer it damaged the most was Peruto, because he had much more to gain from carrying on a dialogue with reporters than did Gallagher. As the trial progressed, Peruto chafed more under the restriction. "There is no reason for the gag order," he grumbled out of Abraham's hearing. "The jury is locked away and can't read the newspapers or watch TV."

The McKenzie fiasco put a definite strain on Peruto's patience; he felt he *had* to say something. During the lunch break, after McKenzie had finished testifying, he slipped furtively down a set of back stairs and filmed a brief interview with local TV reporter David Henry. During the interview the words "McKenzie" and "flake" came up in the same sentence. This would later surface to haunt Peruto. Back in the courtroom Peruto also began having second thoughts about the wisdom of allowing himself to be filmed. He asked Judge Abraham about the order.

"Oh," she said, "I lifted that yesterday. I read it into the record in open court."

Peruto looked puzzled. So did the dozen or so reporters who had been covering the proceedings on a daily basis. Covering a trial can be like watching a football game from the bench: you're close to the action but you can't always see what's going on all over the field. Between sidebar conferences, discussions in chambers, and tidbits thrown into the middle of obtuse legal arguments, one reporter can't always be sure of catching everything. In this case, however, not one of the half-dozen reporters asked had heard Judge Abraham rescind the gag order. This was not a major issue, but it did register as a bleep on some of the reporters' highly tuned antennae.

The gag-order issue was not crucial, but very quickly the subject got more serious. When Peruto called his next witness, Judge Abraham handed down a rigid ruling that seemed to pose a considerable handicap for the defense while immensely benefiting the prosecution.

Chapter 44

As a youth Jack Apsche was a helicopter door gunner in Vietnam. He survived the furious battles in the infamous A Shau Valley. On that Thursday, June 23, as an adult approaching middle age, he almost crashed and burned on a mission in Judge Lynne Abraham's courtroom.

Now a psychologist who specializes in records research, Apsche spent weeks tracing Gary Heidnik's complicated trail, which wound through hospitals on two continents. He came into court prepared to share his findings, which he had gathered in a large, black box he lugged with him to the witness stand. Abraham was not impressed.

As Apsche pulled out his stack of index cards and settled in for what he thought was going to be at least two days of testimony, Judge Abraham launched into an exhaustive explanation of hearsay evidence. In legal terminology, hearsay is evidence that is not within the personal knowledge of a witness. Generally, someone is not allowed to testify to hearsay for two very good reasons: it is inherently unreliable, and the parties involved should have the right to confront those who furnished the information. There are certain exceptions to the rule. Medical records are almost invariably excepted. But this was a special case. Judge Abraham was not going to grant an exception on *Heidnik*'s medical records.

"I can see where his testimony is going to go," Abraham said as Peruto asked his first question, "and I can tell you it isn't going to be acceptable. Even if Dr. Apsche used these records to prepare his diagnosis, they can't be admitted. Opinions, diagnoses, and conclusions will not be admissible."

Peruto was stunned. This was a tremendous and perhaps irreparable blow to his case. His entire defense was based on the insanity plea. With Dr. Clancy McKenzie down the tube, Peruto was going to have to hang his case on his two remaining psychiatric witnesses, one of whom was Apsche. The foundation of his insanity plea was in Apsche's black box—the documentation showing how a whole string of psychiatrists, over a period of a quarter of a century, had found Gary Heidnik to be suffering from a mental illness so severe that his reasoning ability was incapacitated. Ninety percent of Apsche's testimony was scheduled to revolve around those diagnoses. But Abraham was not going to let the jurors hear about them. Peruto didn't know what to say. The only thing he could do was file an objection.

This was an extremely stringent ruling, and a very unusual one. Even more unusual, it appeared to apply only to the defense. Later, when Gallagher wanted to introduce medical records, Abraham permitted it. She herself even read to the jury one record of the type she had prohibited Apsche from discussing. Significantly, that was a report supporting Gallagher's contentions.

Peruto wanted to show that Heidnik's mental problems began when he went on sick call in the U.S. military hospital in Landstuhl. "He went in for a medical problem and he was treated for a mental one," Peruto argued.

"But the doctor who made that diagnosis is not here," said Abraham. It was the last word.

Under her ruling, Apsche would be able to testify only

about Heidnik's admission dates, what symptoms he was complaining about at the time, and what medication he was given. "He can't say what some other doctor concluded," she said. "He doesn't know if that doctor was drunk or deranged."

Further, Apsche would not be allowed to testify about test results listed in the records unless the raw examination data also were included. Armed with raw data, Apsche would be able to interpret the results on his own and not have to depend on someone else's conclusions. The catch was, none of the records contained all the raw data.

Peruto wanted to wail in frustration. He would have to do the best he could within the restrictions.

"In your opinion," he asked Apsche, "did Gary Heidnik know right from wrong?"

"No," replied Apsche, "in my opinion he did not know right from wrong."

"In your opinion, did he know the nature of his acts?"

"He did not know the nature of his acts."

"Was he suffering from a mental disease?"

"Yes."

"What disease?"

"Severe schizophrenia."

Apsche spent the rest of the morning cataloging Heidnik's extensive experiences in mental hospitals stretching from the time he was in the Army virtually until he was arrested. There was one large gap, the period between 1972 and 1978, when Apsche was unable to find any admissions into Heidnik's usual circle of hospitals. Also there was a period between 1983 and 1986 when the records were not clear. During that period Heidnik was admitted to one hospital, walked away, and went to another. The record was confused because the first hospital still carried him on its rolls. Even though he was listed as a patient, he was not physically present in the institution. He could have been anywhere.

Finally, testimony was getting to the real core of the

case: whether Heidnik was insane or whether he was simply faking insanity. Peruto, of course, contended that Heidnik met the criteria for legal insanity. Gallagher, on the other hand, wanted the jury to believe that Heidnik had been faking his mental illness—malingering—since he was a private in the Army. His motive, Gallagher would further assert, was to collect his disability pay and Social Security. In an attempt to strengthen his own position and weaken Gallagher's, Peruto asked Apsche if any of the doctors who had examined Heidnik felt he had been malingering.

"Objection," interjected Gallagher.

"Sustained," said Abraham.

"Are there tests for malingering?" Peruto asked, trying another tack.

"Yes," said Apsche.

"Was Gary Heidnik given these tests?"

"Yes."

Before Peruto could widen this wedge, Judge Abraham cut him off, reminding him about the restriction on test results without the raw data. This touched off another heated discussion, during which Apsche quickly inserted, "No, the evidence does not support the fact that he was malingering." Abraham shot him a forbidding glance.

With tempers running high, she called a lunch break, hoping that feelings would cool over a sandwich.

It worked for a while. For the next hour and a half after the noon recess, the situation was relatively calm while Apsche completed his litany of Heidnik's convoluted paper path.

Things heated up again, however, when Gallagher got the witness on cross-examination.

The DDA zeroed in on the 1983–86 period when Heidnik was difficult to track. When Heidnik was paroled in April 1983, he didn't go on the street. It was a condition of his release that he be admitted to the VA hospital at Coatesville. At some point between then and March 1986, when he was officially discharged from Coatesville, he was not physically at the institution.

Gallagher contended that Heidnik, in fact, left the VA hospital in November 1983.

That wasn't true, Apsche argued. Shuffling through his black box he produced a handful of papers. "Here are nurse's notes showing he *was* in the hospital in '84, '85, and '86," he said.

Gallagher changed direction, attacking Apsche's records as "sketchy."

"You said Heidnik checked himself into the VA hospital at Perry Point, Maryland, in April 1971, because he was depressed over his mother's suicide five days before?" Gallagher asked.

"I didn't say that," Apsche answered. "The record said that."

Digging into a stack of papers, Gallagher handed a sheet to Apsche.

"What was Heidnik's mother's name?" Gallagher queried.

Apsche said he didn't remember.

"It was Ellen Rutledge," said Gallagher. "And what I've just handed you is a copy of a death certificate from Lake County, Ohio, for Ellen Rutledge. It is dated 1970, not 1971." His point was that Heidnik was claiming to suffer depression over his mother's death although it had occurred months previously rather than just a few days before.

Apsche argued that was irrelevant. It's not unusual, he said, for someone to become depressed a year or more after a traumatic event. That is called post-traumatic shock disorder. It is common among Vietnam veterans and others who go through awesome events.

"That makes two errors in your record," Gallagher contended, ignoring Apsche's answer.

"I don't think that's an error," said Apsche.

"I do," interrupted Judge Abraham.

Digging again into his stack of papers, Gallagher produced another document and handed it to Apsche as well. It was a discharge summary from one of Heidnik's admissions to the VA hospital at Coatesville.

Gallagher asked him to read it.

Apsche looked at Abraham and raised his eyebrows. Included in the document was a diagnosis and several specific test scores—two items he had earlier been prohibited from reading.

"You can read it," Abraham said. Apsche did, then tried to read a reentry note that was part of the same record. He wanted to get it before the jury because it indicated Heidnik was readmitted to Coatesville two months later, suffering from delusions and hallucinations. Abraham stopped him.

Apsche complained that the discharge summary was "sketchy."

"Ah," said Gallagher. " 'Sketchy.' "

"That's your word, not mine," Apsche retorted.

"Would you also say that your opinion that this man didn't know right from wrong is also 'sketchy'?"

"No," Apsche answered emphatically.

Chapter 45

June 24, 1988

Chuck Peruto had one big gun. Dr. Kenneth Kool was known throughout the legal community as a courtroom psychiatrist. That is, he is one of a relatively small group of psychiatrists who makes his living by testifying. Sometimes he testifies for the defense. Sometimes he testifies for the prosecution. Over the years, he has appeared at more than a thousand trials. But before the jury could hear from Kool, there were some procedural matters to untangle.

Peruto jumped up as soon as Judge Abraham took her seat and said he was considering calling Vincent Nelson, Josefina Rivera's former boyfriend. Nelson, Peruto said, would testify that he and Rivera discussed electric-shock torture a number of times before Rivera was taken captive by Heidnik. He also would say, Peruto promised, that when Rivera came to him on March 25 she wanted Nelson to go with her so they could rob Heidnik. It was Nelson, not Rivera, who insisted they call the cops, Peruto said. Nelson's availability to testify was not a problem, the defense lawyer added. He was in jail for robbery and illegally carrying a gun. He wasn't going anywhere.

Gallagher objected. "Mr. Nelson's testimony would be irrelevant," he complained.

"No," Judge Abraham responded. "Mr. Peruto can attack Ms. Rivera's credibility. He is entitled to impeach the witness."

But she had more weighty things on her mind. "I'm worried about Dr. Apsche," she said. "Nobody asked him if he was licensed. No one ever verified the authority, the verity of the records. At least, *at least,* he should have attempted to talk to the doctors. My real problem is whether that evidence is even competent. I think I want you gentlemen to go find some [legal] references for your various positions now that the jury has heard the testimony."

"It wasn't objected to," said Peruto. "The Commonwealth has not made a motion to strike it."

"It's the judge who makes that decision," Abraham replied. "It goes to the admissibility of the evidence that he testified to. The question here is not admissibility but competency. I don't have to wait for one of you to make a motion. Otherwise I might just as well wait in my office."

After some discussion of previous cases that might serve as precedent, Gallagher launched an attack on a report Apsche filed before taking the stand. It outlined the areas his testimony would cover.

"His report is filled with errors," the DDA said. "Now we have a report today from Dr. Kool in which he says he met with Dr. Apsche." Gallagher's argument was that Kool relied on Apsche's report, and if Apsche's report was wrong, Kool's testimony would be wrong as well.

Gallagher also complained that Peruto had not turned in reports from his psychiatric witnesses far enough in advance to allow him to study them. "I was given Dr. McKenzie's report ten minutes after he took the stand. Now Mr. Peruto hands in a handwritten report from Dr. Kool. I don't think he has complied with the mandates of this court. Mr. Peruto's actions are not in accordance with the rules, and I ask that Dr. Kool not be allowed to testify. I also ask that Dr. Apsche's testimony be stricken."

"You can cross-examine Dr. Kool on Dr. Apsche's report," Judge Abraham said. "But this just points out an infirmity in our criminal procedure . . . I place that blame on Mr. Peruto. It is a flagrant abuse of my orders."

But that was still not what really worried her. After perusing Kool's report, she said she feared that his testimony was going to infringe on the jury's prerogatives.

Kool's handwritten, three-page document, dated the previous day, addressed some touchy issues. Three, to be specific. Insanity. Diminished capacity. Guilty but insane. All different concepts but all dealing with a defendant's mental state at the time a crime was committed. Peruto's defense involved all of these concepts. He was covering all the bases.

Diminished capacity, or diminished responsibility, is recognized as a defense to a criminal charge in many states, including Pennsylvania. When making such a plea, the defense admits that the accused is legally sane but is substantially lacking in mental capacity. As interpreted in the courtroom, it means that the defense may be admitting that the defendant is *not* insane but neither does he have the mental capacity to premeditate. That is, to plan a murder. Therefore, lacking the ability to form premeditation, he cannot be found guilty of first degree (that is, intentional) murder. In Pennsylvania a defendant can be sentenced to death only if convicted of first-degree murder. Any other murder conviction carries a maximum sentence of life in prison.

If Peruto could convince the jury that Heidnik did not have the mental capacity to plan a murder, he could only be convicted of a charge lesser than first degree. That would save him from execution.

However, he was not going to get any support for diminished capacity from Kool. The psychiatrist's report was unequivocal on the issue. "Diminished capacity is not to be considered in this case," he wrote.

Guilty but mentally ill is a separate concept. Diminished capacity concedes a person is sane. So does guilty but mentally ill, but it has the added acknowledgment that a person *is* suffering from a severe mental illness. While this illness may not rise to the level of legal insanity, the very fact that he has this illness means that he cannot be held legally responsible for a crime to the same extent as someone who is not mentally ill. Generally, a person found guilty but mentally ill is treated at a hospital instead of being sent to prison. Once his mental illness has been cured, he begins serving his prison term.

This concept is causing quite a bit of trouble in the legal community. No one, it seems, has been able to get a good handle on it. Just about every guilty-but-mentally-ill law that has been passed has received serious complaints from one quarter or another. Legal scholars agree that the concept is good but the execution is flawed.

Just as Peruto could not look to Kool to support a diminished capacity argument, neither could he ask the psychiatrist to back a guilty-but-mentally-ill one.

"I am of the opinion that the criteria for guilty but mentally ill are not met," Kool wrote. "That finding requires a capacity Heidnik did not possess at the time. I find no evidence that he could discern he was delusional, no evidence of mental capacity to reflect upon, recognize, or have clear cognition of right and wrong or nature and quality" (knowing what he was doing).

Both diminished capacity and guilty-but-mentally-ill findings differ from a straight insanity verdict. If a person is acquitted by reason of insanity, he can be committed to a mental institution but cannot be held responsible for his crime. Once he is declared cured of his mental illness or is no longer thought to be a danger to the public, he can be released. There is no prison sentence attached.

Peruto *was* going to get support from Kool on Heidnik's alleged insanity. Strong support.

"It is my opinion," the psychiatrist wrote, "that during that [November–March] period, Mr. Heidnik was suffering from an exacerbation of his long-standing schizophrenia, and it was of such intensity that it denied him the mental capacity to know the nature and quality of his behaviors and denied him the mental capacity to know right from wrong.

"The basis for this opinion is that he was reacting to systematized delusion and had no conscious awareness of, nor insight into, the fact that he was psychotic at the time and that his distorted perceptions and behaviors were a direct product of that psychosis. His 'reality' was a delusion. Not having the mental capacity to recognize that fact, he reacted to what his psychosis caused him to perceive as real. The psychosis denied him the mental capacity to knowingly reflect and make informed decisions. His lifestyle was bizarre, chaotic, and regressed under the dominance of a profound psychosis . . . I am of the opinion that this is a case that meets the criteria for [insanity]."

That was pretty strong stuff. But it was not what had Abraham concerned. She was worried that Kool's testimony was going to be too authoritative; that it was going to confuse the jury.

"In looking at Dr. Kool's report," she said. "The problem I have is that he is saying that evidence of guilty but mentally ill is not here. I don't think it's appropriate for him to tell that to the jury. The doctor can say that the defendant was not suffering from a mental illness under the statute, but he cannot say the jury cannot return a verdict [to the contrary]. That usurps the function of the jury . . . How can he say a man is crazy, but not guilty but mentally ill? That's going to confuse the jury."

Peruto bounded to his feet. "He goes beyond guilty but

mentally ill. He does not say Gary Heidnik doesn't suffer from mental illness."

"It causes the jury too much confusion," said Abraham. "I can't let Dr. Kool tell the jury they can't find him guilty but mentally ill. He may *not* intrude into the fact-finding function."

Peruto disagreed. "He *can* intrude because he is an expert."

"No," Judge Abraham snapped. "An expert may never intrude. He can give his opinion and that's all."

"He just wants to say it goes beyond guilty but mentally ill," Peruto argued.

"He may *not* overrule the legislature," Abraham said. "The legislature has put that in the jury's prerogative."

That was the end of the discussion. Peruto sat down.

But Abraham was not through with the defense lawyer. She had seen the morning *Inquirer,* which had a story quoting Peruto as calling Dr. Clancy McKenzie a flake. "I have a grave problem with a lawyer calling his own witness a flake," she said, glaring at Peruto. "I don't want either of you," she added, including Gallagher in the order, "calling McKenzie a flake to Dr. Kool."

The discussion had taken an hour and fifteen minutes. The jury, in the meantime, was kept sitting in an anteroom—wondering, no doubt, what was going on that they were not privy to. When they were called in, though, they looked chipper and ready to work. A cool front had swept through during the night, clearing the blanket of smog. It was still warm in Room 653 because the air-conditioning had not yet caught up, but the inside temperature would drop during the day. That may have been due, in part, to Kool, who was every bit as calm and collected as his name indicated. He was a pro. Gallagher wasn't going to rattle him.

Chapter 46

Kenneth Kool is stamped in the mold of Gary Cooper when Gary Cooper was in his prime: tall, slim, laconic, unflappable. As a courtroom veteran, he was unintimidated by his surroundings. He looked more at home behind the bar than either of the lawyers facing him.

In his radio announcer's voice, speaking distinctly and confidently, he said he spent about seven hours examining Gary Heidnik and another three with Jack Apsche, going over Heidnik's voluminous records.

"Have you reached an opinion about Mr. Heidnik?" Peruto asked overanxiously.

Slow down, warned Judge Abraham: "Lay your foundation first."

In response to a series of questions from Peruto, Kool said he had carefully studied Heidnik's medical history and had reached a conclusion based on the information he had and his experience studying mentally-ill defendants. "I don't know every element [of his personality], but I have what I assume to be the highlights," he said.

"From November to March, did he appreciate the nature and quality of his acts?" Peruto queried.

"No," said Kool, adding that Heidnik also did not have the capacity to know right from wrong.

"He could drive a car," said Peruto. "Did that make any difference?"

"No."

"If I told you he placed a body in New Jersey, would that change your opinion?"

"No."

Under questioning from Peruto and Judge Abraham, Kool repeated the details he had already outlined in his report: that Heidnik was delusional and did not know it; that he was psychotic; that he had an unbalanced perception of reality; that his lifestyle was bizarre and regressed.

"What is a delusion?" Peruto asked.

"A delusion is an unreality perceived by the victim of it to be a reality," answered Kool.

"Are you aware of his goal?"

"I'm aware of his delusional goal," Kool began. "He had evolved a paranoid and grandiose delusion that God wanted him to produce a number of children. He looked upon it as a partnership with God. This was a fixed delusion, and he had it for a long time. It was totally out of context with reality. He believed that if he were detected, he would be prevented from carrying out this delusion."

Peruto asked Kool if he thought Heidnik knew what he was doing was unlawful.

"He had some awareness of man's law, what the laws of the Commonwealth were, but he saw God's law as superior. He did not have the capacity to reflect upon these things."

"Did you see any progression in his medical records?"

"Yes, I did. I saw the predictors of what would occur. The fact that he kidnapped a young lady and kept her in a closet in his basement was one of those predictors. His writing the parole board and signing the letter 'G. M. Kill' was another thing I saw as an indicator. Another was his profound reaction to the loss of his known children. The neglect of his wife when she was pregnant . . .

history indicates all the elements were there for a tragedy."

"You would agree," interrupted Abraham, "that two psychiatrists can disagree, and one can be just as qualified as another?"

"Yes," answered Kool.

"Would it change your opinion if Gary Heidnik had been mute with you?" Peruto asked.

"No," said Kool, "but it would change the basis on which I formed my opinion."

"Would it change your opinion if I told you that the first thing he wanted to do after dumping Deborah Dudley's body was to buy a newspaper to check his stocks?"

"No."

Peruto ticked off several things that would seem to indicate that Heidnik had periods of apparent normality and asked Kool how this squared with an opinion of insanity.

"His psychoses are primarily in the areas of reproduction—having babies and completing his pact with God," replied Kool. "He does not have it in areas that are not conflicting."

"You often see malingerers, do you not?" asked Peruto, changing course.

"Yes."

"Did you find any history of malingering throughout his history?"

"No," answered Kool. "I'm of the opinion that he is not sane and has not been so over the years. There are things that auger against claims of his malingering. Look at how many times he wanted to remain in hospitals when they wanted him to leave. His writing the parole board. His habit of stockpiling medicine. His remaining mute. There was never anything to be gained by malingering over all those years. There was no advantage; no secondary gain."

* * *

When Charles Gallagher took over on cross-examination, his approach was quite different than it had been with McKenzie and Apsche. Gallagher was almost deferential to Kool.

"You saw no evidence of malingering, right?"

"Right."

"Did you compare his hospital admissions with the dates he filed claims with the Social Security Administration and the VA?"

"I don't remember those specifically."

Gallagher outlined the circumstances of Heidnik's discharge from the Army and how his pension benefits were increased from ten percent to a hundred percent.

Before he could get deep into his examination, however, Peruto asked Judge Abraham to excuse the jury so he could discuss something else. The issue was Vincent Nelson. Peruto said he had dropped his plans to call him to the stand.

"Mr. Peruto was concerned [Nelson] was going to commit perjury in order to aggrandize himself," Abraham announced after a brief sidebar conference.

"He may have been seriously mistaken [about some of his claims]," Peruto added.

With the jury back in, Gallagher resumed his questioning of Kool. First, though, he handed Kool a sheet of paper and asked him if he had ever seen it before.

"No," said Kool. "I did not see this."

Under Gallagher's prompting, Kool read extensively from the document, which dealt with Heidnik's examinations at military hospitals in Germany and the United States. Included was a diagnosis by an Army doctor that said Heidnik had a schizophrenic personality but was not psychotic.

It was striking that Judge Abraham allowed Kool to

read a previous doctor's diagnosis—at Gallagher's urging —while she would not permit Apsche to read diagnoses at Peruto's request. Asked about this during the lunch break, Abraham said: "This was information he had not seen, and it might make him change his opinion. This was a different witness. This was a doctor who had spent seven hours examining Heidnik and he testified that he based his opinion in part on records. This was a record he didn't have. This was a whole different kettle of fish."

Despite Peruto's objections, all of which were overruled by Judge Abraham, Gallagher presented document after document to Kool and asked him to read from them. One was a report of a security check done on Heidnik in 1965 in response to an application for employment. Gallagher presented this because he wanted to get on the record that Heidnik had trained for several months as a psychiatric nurse with the VA.

"If someone has an IQ of 148, what does that mean to you?" Gallagher asked.

"IQ scores are relative. Ninety to 110 is average; 148 is very high."

"How about 130?"

"That's superior to very superior."

"On May 24, 1978, Gary Heidnik was evaluated . . ." Gallagher began.

"Objection," yelled Peruto.

"Overruled," said Abraham.

". . . and he had a score of 120 on the verbal section, 127 on performance, and 130 full scale."

Again Judge Abraham had allowed Gallagher to present the same type of evidence she had forbidden Apsche and Peruto from proffering. She told Apsche he could refer to test results only if he had all the raw data and scored them himself. She did not ask Gallagher if he had the raw data. He did not volunteer the information.

Changing direction, Gallagher asked Kool if he agreed with McKenzie's theory of the cause of schizophrenia.

"Very, very few psychiatrists share the theory that early life experiences are the sole factor in determining schizophrenia," Kool said, wording his reply carefully. "Many feel it is primarily a genetic illness . . . [but] all the votes are not in yet. Like cancer, it is a very complicated phenomenon and is not curable. Medication complicates it. There is a justifiable place in psychiatry for all these theories . . . we don't have a real handle on schizophrenia yet."

Gallagher asked: What percentage of psychiatrists agreed with McKenzie that early-life experiences were paramount?

"Much, much less than five percent regard it as the exclusive cause," Kool said.

Gallagher repeated Heidnik's pension-benefit history and asked if he thought that indicated that Heidnik was malingering.

"No," said Kool. "In my opinion he has a major mental illness."

"Do you think he was telling you the truth when you examined him?"

"Yes."

Gallagher wanted to know if he was certain.

"I can't read minds," Kool replied. "I'm giving you my best opinion. I can't tell if someone is lying."

Still pursuing the issue, Gallagher detailed Heidnik's frequent transfers between mental hospitals when he was serving his prison sentence for his attack on Alberta Davidson.

"I don't have any knowledge of this," said Kool.

"Doesn't all this indicate to you that he is a malingerer?"

"No," Kool said forcefully.

With a nod to Judge Abraham, Gallagher indicated he had finished his cross-examination of Kool. After the trial, on the late-night talk show with Larry King, Gallagher would brag about how he "demolished" all three of the defense's psychiatric witnesses. If Kool, for one, had been demolished, he didn't act it.

Since Kool was the last defense witness, Gallagher began his rebuttal after lunch. His first witness was Dr. Robert Sadoff, another courtroom professional on the same level as Kool. Like Kool, Sadoff testifies for either side. This time he was lined up with the prosecution. Like Kool, he was virtually unflappable.

Chapter 47

Charles Gallagher yanked at the back of his jacket and called his witness in a loud, clear voice: "Robert Sadoff." A neatly dressed man with short, brown hair and a relaxed manner walked briskly to the witness stand and raised his right hand. Like Kenneth Kool, Sadoff had been in so many courtrooms, he probably carried his own Bible.

"I've testified in federal and state courts in twenty states," he admitted modestly when Gallagher questioned him to establish his credentials. "I've testified before a Senate committee to discuss what should be done with people who are found guilty but mentally ill." And Gallagher, anticipating an insanity defense by Heidnik's lawyer, signed him up to testify for the prosecution within weeks after Heidnik's arrest.

Despite the long-term commitment, Sadoff wasn't able to get much out of Heidnik. He spent about twenty minutes with him before he gave up in disgust. Heidnik refused to talk. The two never exchanged a word.

It didn't matter, though, he told Gallagher. He fell back on Heidnik's medical records, his personal business records, police records, and testimony from other expert witnesses.

"What is the legal definition of insanity?" was Gallagher's first question.

"The difference between someone who is insane and someone who is mentally ill is that the insane person doesn't know the nature and quality of his act and he doesn't know right from wrong."

"Did Gary Heidnik know what he was doing when he picked up those girls?"

"In my opinion, he did. He wasn't just grabbing people off the street as a person with a seventeen-month-old brain would do." He couldn't resist the dig at McKenzie.

"Did he pick them up to satisfy his sexual desire?"

"I'm not so sure that's wrong. Men do it all the time."

"Did he know what he was doing when he choked and cuffed them?"

"In my opinion, yes."

"Did he know it was wrong?"

"In my opinion, he did know."

For the next ten minutes Gallagher led Sadoff through a series of similar questions covering all of Heidnik's major acts during the four-month period. Sadoff answered each one affirmatively, prefacing each answer with, "In my opinion . . ."

"Based on your review, do you have an opinion about Gary Heidnik?"

"I think he is probably schizophrenic. I would agree with those who call him that."

"Is he a malingerer?"

"At times he has shown evidence of exaggerating his mental illness . . . of being manipulative."

Gallagher asked if his mutism was a sign of mental illness or a sign of malingering.

"I think he was exaggerating his mutism, for whatever reasons," Sadoff answered. "He would choose not to talk, to present a psychotic image to the doctors, but behind the scenes he was doing what he always did."

The DDA asked if Sadoff thought Heidnik had been

malingering when he presented himself for admission to the Maryland hospital in 1971 soon after he had asked the Social Security Administration to reconsider its action on his request for benefits.

"It was either incredibly coincidental, which I don't think it was, or this was a very bright man who decided to go to Maryland where he could have a bright new start [with a new Social Security office]."

He added that he also thought Heidnik was malingering when he was serving his prison sentence. His motive was to stay in mental hospitals because it was more pleasant than being in the prison's general population. No matter where he was transferred within the system, Sadoff said, Heidnik always managed to let his stock broker know where he was.

"Is it possible for someone to fake mental illness?"

"I think one can fake mental illness easier than insanity. Mental illness is not hard to fake."

"In your opinion did he have a major mental illness that caused him *not* to know the nature and quality of his acts?"

"Maybe he had a major mental illness," Sadoff said, "but the evidence indicates he was not so deprived of his reason that he did not know the nature and quality of his acts."

Gallagher asked Sadoff if he thought Heidnik should be held responsible for his acts.

"You have to hold a person responsible or not responsible," said Sadoff. "There is nothing to indicate that Heidnik did not know what he was doing was wrong at the time he was doing it."

Just as Gallagher had been unable to shake Kool, Peruto was unable to shake Sadoff. In response to a question from Peruto if he had ever been wrong in his opinions, Sadoff calmly admitted that in some cases the courts had found differently. "But I'm not sure it was my mistake or someone else's."

Although it was only 3:45, forty-five minutes before the usual quitting time, Judge Abraham was so pleased with how rapidly the trial was progressing, she decided to knock off for the weekend. While she initially planned Saturday sessions, things were going so smoothly she cancelled that idea.

Before she adjourned, however, she picked up a document and read into the record the results of an IQ test given to Heidnik on March 16, 1987, nine days before he was arrested. The test was part of the battery ordered by Judge Levin in family court. She said Heidnik scored 148.

By doing this, Judge Abraham violated her own prohibition on test results levied when Apsche tried to read some scores to the jury. She also did not say that the test on which Heidnik scored a 148 is generally regarded by testing experts as inferior to the type of test on which Heidnik twice scored a 130. Apsche was trying to get the 130 score before the jury as well as the results of the tests Heidnik took which purported to show he was not faking his symptoms.

Judge Abraham also announced that she had decided not to erase Apsche's testimony. Doing that, she said, "may strike a blow to the defense that they needn't suffer." Peruto didn't say thank you.

Chapter 48

Once the psychiatrists were through with their main testimony, the tension in the room lifted like a hot-air balloon. The end was in sight now and everyone seemed to be relieved. When the jury was called in, the change was evident. They had more spring in their step and looked almost festive. Six of the men wore ties. Gary Heidnik felt it too. Earlier he showed up wearing a blue, Oxford cloth, long-sleeve shirt carefully buttoned at the wrist. It was too large by several sizes, but it was clean and pressed. It was the first time in fifteen months he had not worn his faded Hawaiian shirt during a public appearance. Even the weather was cooperating. Another cool front moved in over the weekend, and the temperature inside Room 653 was the most comfortable it had been since the proceeding started.

Before the jury was summoned, however, there were—as usual—several procedural matters to haggle over.

Charles Gallagher told Judge Abraham that among the mop-up rebuttal witnesses he intended to call was someone to testify that Heidnik had bars put on the downstairs windows of his house in 1985. This indicated, he said, that Heidnik was planning his abductions even then.

Abraham shook her head. "I think you're going way

overboard," she said. It was one of her rare rebukes to the prosecution.

Gallagher also wanted to recall police lieutenant James Hansen to testify about some books police recovered in their search of Heidnik's house.

"What kind of books?" Abraham asked.

"One was *Criminal Law in a Nutshell*," said Gallagher. "One was on abnormal psychology. One was on how to buy stocks. There was one about the Pinkerton detective agency, and there was a New York phone book."

Peruto objected. "Some of those might be prejudicial to the defendant," he argued. "Plus, there is no indication when he got the books. If the prosecution can be selective, I'd like to show what else was in the house."

"Fine," Gallagher responded. "I'll bring the other dozen boxes or so over here too."

"What is the relevance?" Abraham wanted to know.

"To show he is a malingerer," said Gallagher.

In the end Gallagher did not introduce the books. Nor did he call the workman who put the bars on the window.

But the DDA was not the only one running into roadblocks over witnesses. Peruto told Judge Abraham he would like to call Betty Heidnik, but Abraham balked.

"There's no benefit to your client to have this woman produced," the judge said. "Your client is very dangerous to women, and this witness could be too prejudicial. I will not let her talk about how dangerous she thought he was."

"As an attorney, I feel it is not prejudicial," Peruto argued. "I think it's helpful."

"It renders your defense useless," Abraham countered. "It shows he was cold and calculating. It doesn't help him at all. All it proves is that he is a cold-blooded killer."

"It is prejudicial *not* to let it in," Peruto persisted.

"There goes your insanity defense then," said Judge Abraham. "You might as well plead guilty. It shows he is a cold-blooded, calculated killer. It doesn't advance your theory of the case. It shuts it down."

"If the Commonwealth is allowed to introduce doctors and reports . . . I can't take it in a vacuum," Peruto said. "The jury has to have it all. They have to have the whole thing."

After all the argument, Betty Heidnik was not called. On reflection, Peruto conceded she could only have damaged his case. Not only could she testify about how he abused her, but her recitation of Heidnik's promiscuity would wreck his argument that he was having sex with the women in his basement only to reproduce.

That did not mean there was a shortage of last-minute witnesses. In a blur nine people trooped to the stand as prosecution rebuttal witnesses to bolster Gallagher's contention that Gary Heidnik was sane. Among them was Heidnik's stock broker, one of Heidnik's former girlfriends, the sales manager from the Cadillac agency, the psychologist who tested Heidnik in March 1987—just before his arrest—and a psychiatrist from a VA outpatient clinic who saw Heidnik three times during the four-month period he was holding the captives.

When Robert Kirkpatrick took the stand, Heidnik underwent a remarkable transformation. So far during the trial Heidnik seemed to exhibit little interest in the testimony or the arguments. Occasionally he conversed with Peruto, but for the most part he simply stared at the wall behind the judge's bench and rocked back and forth on the back legs of his straight-backed chair. But when his former broker took the stand, Heidnik became animated. When Merrill Lynch's representative spoke, Heidnik listened. Intently.

Kirkpatrick was Heidnik's broker because he happened to answer the telephone when Heidnik called one

day in December 1974. The broker said the caller introduced himself as "Bishop Heidnik" and said he was interested in opening an account. Several weeks later he
followed up the call with a letter. Enclosed was a check
for $1,500. The account was opened on March 21, 1975,
in the name of the United Church of the Ministers of
God.

Over the next dozen years, Kirkpatrick said, he saw
Heidnik only about four times in person because he normally handled affairs by telephone or through the mail.

"Did anyone else control this account?" Gallagher
asked.

"No," answered Kirkpatrick.

The broker produced a sheet showing how the account
grew progressively larger. By October 27, 1979, the balance was $21,000. By July 31, 1982, it had increased ten-
fold, to $256,000. By the following May it had taken
another large jump, to $361,000. For the next couple of
years it fluctuated slightly. But by November 28, 1986—
two days after Heidnik captured Josefina Rivera and the
day before he took Sandra Lindsay—the balance was
$545,000.

During most of this time, Kirkpatrick testified,
Heidnik was an enthusiastic player and kept in touch
frequently. In May 1983 he wrote Kirkpatrick and reminded him not to forget the church's thirty-five percent
discount. At another time he chided Kirkpatrick for not
transferring $60,000 from an inactive account to an ac-
tive one so it would draw interest.

"Did he ever lose money on Crazy Eddie stock?" Gallagher asked.

"No, he did not," Kirkpatrick answered.

"What kind of investor was he?"

Peruto objected, but Judge Abraham overruled.

"An astute investor," the broker said.

Kirkpatrick severely damaged the defense. The picture
he painted of Heidnik was of a bright, fervent investor

who knew what he was about. The best Peruto could do was try to show that underneath, Heidnik was not as rational as he appeared on the surface.

"Did he ever tell you he was raising ten babies in his basement?"

Kirkpatrick admitted he had not.

"If he had, what would you have done?"

"I would have reported it to my superiors immediately and recommended that the account be closed."

"Every time you saw him, was he wearing the same clothing?"

"You mean the same style?"

"No, I mean the same clothing."

"I have no idea," Kirkpatrick said, explaining that there was as large a gap as six years between their meetings.

Peruto also wanted to clarify the Crazy Eddie issue.

"When you said he didn't lose any money on Crazy Eddie, you mean he didn't sell it at a loss?"

"Yes."

"But if he had sold it, he would have been down considerably?"

"Yes."

Kirkpatrick put a big dent in Peruto's insanity plea. So, too, did Gallagher's next witness, a former girlfriend named Shirley Carter.

A forty-year-old black woman suffering from cerebral palsy, Carter testified she had a sexual relationship with Heidnik extending from the period before he went to prison until not long after he got out in 1983. She testified that Heidnik was very intelligent, frequently telling her how to invest her money and what stocks to buy. "He even told me how he set up a church so he wouldn't have to pay taxes," Carter said.

"Did he ever do anything bizarre?" Gallagher asked.

"Not really," Carter answered.

Carter's most damning evidence against Heidnik, however, would not be brought out. In a folder on the table in
front of him, Gallagher had a copy of a ten-page handwritten letter from Heidnik to Carter. It was dated June
9, 1982. At the time, Heidnik was still serving his prison
sentence.

Beginning, "Dear Sweety bun," the letter dealt mostly
with financial issues. It read:

> Say things go good for us, I get paroled and sent
> to Coatesville. You then move out there, have the
> two children we're planning on (Lisa and Gary Jr.)
> . . . when we achieve this situation, it involves an
> increase in our income of about $700 a month . . .
> The good part is that this is *extra* money. I'll still
> continue getting my $1,800 a month also. That
> doesn't even count the money from the stock mar-
> ket. That will give us a *tax exempt* income of over
> $70,000 a year. WOW! If you figure we're also get-
> ting other benefits, like free health care, that brings
> it up to about $75,000 a year. WOW! Since this is
> all tax exempt, it's equivalent to someone else mak-
> ing and paying taxes on about $110,000 a year.
> WOW!! This isn't even taking into consideration
> other plans I have for increasing our income (like a
> couple of choice boarders, getting welfare or SSI,
> who will also be willing to help out around the
> house with things like cooking and cleaning . . .).
> No wonder you don't have any interest in working.
> In many ways, including financial, it seems our
> union was made in heaven . . .

The rest of the letter dealt with problems Carter was
having with her mother, a used car Heidnik wanted to
buy for her, how he thought he was given an unjust
prison sentence, his scores on the IQ tests ("I passed with
a 130 score, which is pretty high"), and about how he

had applied for a department-store credit card. "If I get it, you'll get a nice little present and Price [Carter's son] will get a basketball set. It includes a basketball and pump even. So if you get a basketball, I'm sure you'll know it's for Price and not for you (he, he, he)."

Gallagher had wanted to introduce the letter, but Judge Abraham had ruled it was too remote to apply to the current case. While it would have tainted Heidnik's insanity plea in one way, it would have helped in another. Even then Heidnik showed a preoccupation with having children. More than once in the letter he talked about their plans to produce a son and daughter. ". . . Lisa and Gary Jr. I like writing their names," he penned. He also laid down a plan he would follow once he got out: buy a house, find a couple of boarders drawing Social Security and use their income as well as their manual labor. Conceivably, Apsche or Kool could have argued convincingly that these were still more predictors.

Chapter 49

At first Dr. Richard Hole didn't want to talk about Gary Heidnik. "Don't worry about the doctor-patient privilege," Judge Abraham told the psychiatrist from a Philadelphia VA outpatient clinic. "You can feel perfectly free to answer the questions."

On the third Wednesday of December 1986, Hole said nervously, Heidnik unexpectedly came back to the clinic for treatment after a ten-month lapse. When he left, he was participating in group-therapy sessions and taking 200 milligrams a day of Thorazine.

Hole said Heidnik was not complaining of any symptoms "nor did he show manifestations of ongoing or poorly treated schizophrenic illness."

When asked to define Heidnik's problem, Hole said he was a paranoid schizophrenic, but his illness appeared to be under control.

"I asked him if he was depressed," Hole said, "and he denied it." He also denied he was suicidal, paranoid, hallucinatory, or delusional. "He essentially denied all psychiatric symptomatology," Hole said. Nevertheless, the psychiatrist prescribed more Thorazine.

In January and February Heidnik returned and his condition appeared not to have changed. That was the last personal contact Hole had with him, although he said Heidnik telephoned in mid-March. He wanted Hole to write a letter to the court asking for a renewal of visiting rights with his eight-year-old daughter.

During cross-examination Hole denied that Heidnik exhibited a common symptom of schizophrenia, the numbness of spirit called the "flat affect."

"If he had, he wouldn't have given a big smile to the other patients he hadn't seen in ten months."

"Did you perform any tests to show he was not taking his medication?" Peruto asked.

"No," Hole replied, adding that Heidnik did not show any signs of a "poorly controlled schizophrenic," so he assumed he was taking his Thorazine.

If he had no symptoms, Peruto asked, why did he need medication?

"To prevent an outbreak or a relapse of the illness," Hole replied.

Earlier Gallagher had proffered the theory that Heidnik had not taken his medication (evidenced by the fact that a considerable amount of Thorazine was found in Heidnik's house after the arrest) because it would reduce his sex drive. Peruto asked Hole if that were true.

The amount of Thorazine he had prescribed was unlikely to impair a healthy young man's sex drive, Hole said.

"Hold on," Judge Abraham interrupted. "That's not the reason he was called. He was called only to talk about his experiences with Heidnik between December and February."

"Four times a day with four different women?" Peruto said, plunging on.

"Objection," yelled Gallagher.

"Sustained," snapped Abraham.

"Do you have any reason to believe he was malingering or faking it?"

"Based on the time frame of December, January, and February, I would say no."

"He was not faking his medical symptoms?"

"Correct."

The final major prosecution witness was Eva Wojcie-chowski, the court psychologist who examined Heidnik on Judge Levin's orders. The examination took place on March 16, 1987, some five weeks after Sandra Lindsay died and two days before Deborah Dudley was electrocuted.

Although he scored a 148 on the IQ test, Wojciechowski explained that the type of test given him was not as authoritative as the test that is usually given, called the Wechsler Adult Intelligence Scale, or WAIS. When Heidnik was evaluated in 1978 after being charged with abducting Alberta Davidson, and three other times as well, he was given the WAIS. Twice he had scores of 130.

Gallagher asked the psychologist how common a score of 148 was.

Only one half of one percent of the population scores in that range, she said. Such a score is near genius.

Gallagher dwelled on the score at length, implying that Heidnik was too smart to be crazy.

When Peruto got the witness, his first question was aimed at undermining the foundation of Gallagher's theory that Heidnik's mental illness was an elaborate hoax.

"Is there any indication he was faking?" Peruto queried.

"No," Wojciechowski said decisively.

"What was the purpose of the tests?"

"To see if he was employable."

"Was he?"

"I didn't think so," replied Wojciechowski. "[The tests showed] he has very strong, aggressive, violent tendencies, and he is apt to go off if he doesn't get what he wants."

"What do you think he wanted?"

"I think he wanted custody of his son."

* * *

Although Gallagher had called more witnesses than expected, the trial was winding down on schedule. Peruto planned to recall Kenneth Kool on Tuesday to counter Sadoff, and that would be the end of testimony. After that the two lawyers would present their closing arguments. The jury would have the case by Wednesday afternoon.

Chapter 50

June 28, 1988

Chuck Peruto's first question to Kenneth Kool was totally predictable. What in the world, he wanted to know, does IQ have to do with schizophrenia?

"Nothing at all," Kool answered calmly. "Schizophrenia is a major mental illness that can develop in any human being."

"When Dr. Hole testified yesterday, he said he asked Heidnik if he was delusional. Is that a proper question?"

"No," Kool said with a fleeting grin. "Asking a schizophrenic if he is delusional is kind of ludicrous. They will say no because they perceive their delusion to be reality. They will deny it. Asking them that is an exercise in futility."

"What about malingering [when he was being interviewed by Hole]?"

"If he wanted to malinger, he would have told the doctor he had all those mental problems."

Peruto asked Kool if he placed any significance on the fact that the Thorazine prescribed by Hole was found in Heidnik's house.

"That makes it even more likely that without his medication his fixed delusional system was operating," Kool stated.

How could Kool explain Heidnik's different behavior?

Peruto asked. How could he do some things—negotiate for a car, buy stocks—and act the way he did at other times?

"His delusions were not involved with buying cars or stocks," answered Kool. "They were in the area of his relationships with people, particularly women and children. There you can see a marked contrast which is explainable in terms of his psychosis."

As soon as he got the witness, Gallagher jumped to his feet. "So Gary Heidnik had selective delusions?" he asked.

"No," replied Kool. "That is not the word. 'Selective' suggests an ability to turn it on and off. Heidnik had no control."

Gallagher: "His delusional spigot was on when he was in the house and off when he was out buying cars?"

Kool: "This man did not reveal his delusional behavior to other people. It fits. He was hiding his behavior the same way he did the bodies."

Gallagher hammered at the delusional concept, bringing in Heidnik's church, his testimony during the support hearing before Judge Levin, and his treatment at Farview when he was under the prison sentence.

"Isn't this man pretending?" he asked pugnaciously.

"Nooo waaaay," Kool shot back.

When Kool stepped down, Judge Abraham sent the jury out of the room. She wanted to lay down the ground rules for closing arguments.

"I don't want counsel to talk about penalty," she said. "That doesn't mean you, Mr. Peruto, can't mention guilty but mentally ill."

Turning to Gallagher. "Here's something to remember. You can say Mr. Heidnik has been released from mental institutions twenty-two times, ergo, he might be released again."

To both of them: "I don't want any inflammatory language. Don't bring up other cases. Keep to the evidence, logical inferences, and your position in regard to the case."

Judge Abraham said Peruto would go first. He objected, but was overruled. In Pennsylvania it is customary for the prosecution to have the last say. The rationale is that it is fair because the prosecution has the burden of proof. However, many legal scholars consider such a situation a tremendous advantage for the prosecution. Each lawyer could talk as long as he wanted, Abraham said.

Peruto took the floor at 11:06. He was wearing a luxurious light-gray suit and a red-and-gray rep tie. His blue shirt had the initials ACP embroidered in dark thread, running vertically down the front, parallel to the placket.

"The question is not whether Gary Heidnik did these heinous acts," he said softly, "but whether or not he was insane. We're not contesting that these women were raped, that these women were kidnapped, that these women were killed. What we're here to determine is the level of culpability of the defendant. Even though we have conceded that these acts took place, we are not conceding first-degree murder—the specific intent to kill."

Walking briskly back and forth before the jurors, he suggested they consider what the prosecution was asking them to believe.

"Let's say he's a malingerer. A faker. That he went into the Army with plans to develop a paranoid schizophrenic personality so one day he could make a living that way . . . Could he fool all those doctors all the time? Could he fake mental illness—schizophrenia—for twenty-five years? You have to believe that. You have to believe he did this for twenty-five years so when he got caught building his family in his basement, he could say he was insane. That's the prosecution's case. Does that make sense?"

Peruto's voice rose emotionally. The jurors remained

stone-faced, but they followed him carefully with their eyes.

"What was Gary Heidnik's purpose? His purpose was to raise ten kids, not to kill anybody." He was punishing the women for disobeying him, he said, not trying to murder them. "Third-degree murder is reckless disregard for human life. This is a classic case of third degree."

One of the women was retarded, he said. One was illiterate. Three were prostitutes. "As sick as it is, these were his chosen people. These were the girls he wanted to reproduce with. Is that sane? It's a case of Dr. Jekyll and Mr. Heidnik. Isn't it more likely he's insane than not?

"What kind of mentality does it take to have human flesh in front of you. A human being. And to cut through that body. To cut through flesh. To cut through bone, and to take some of those body parts and wrap them up and put them in the freezer. And then to cook some and feed it to the others? Who was he trying to impress with that delusion? The body was wrapped, but he wasn't."

Sandra Lindsay's mother, who was sitting in the front row of the packed courtroom, began sobbing. Another relative took her arm and led her out.

Peruto seethed when he talked about Josefina Rivera. "She was feeding a sick mind . . . she knew he was sick and she turned that to her advantage . . . Listen to Lisa [Thomas]: she said Rivera was laughing about beating the others. That she did it with or without Gary. Did Lisa make that up? What is her motivation? Ladies and gentlemen, I am going to argue to you that Josefina Rivera acted criminally . . . that she did a couple of things that went too far. She was putting sugar on his plan."

Switching back to Heidnik, he summed up. "I don't want a verdict based on sympathy," he said. "Nor do I want one based on prejudice . . . I want you to find him not guilty based on insanity."

Peruto sat down. It was 11:51. He had spoken for exactly forty-five minutes.

Judge Abraham gave the jury a brief recess, and then it was Gallagher's turn. It was four minutes after noon when he began.

Standing solemnly before the jury, Gallagher searched his left jacket pocket, then folded his hands in front of him. "I want you to rely upon your good old-fashioned common sense," he said quietly. "Rely upon your powers of observation. Go over the evidence with me."

Turning quickly, he raised his arm and pointed at Heidnik, who was, as usual, staring at the rear wall, apparently oblivious to the proceedings.

"This man," Gallagher said, his voice rising, "repeated sadistic and malicious acts upon six victims. He planned it. He did it, and he concealed it. Ladies and gentlemen, I submit to you—make no mistake about it—that this man committed murder in the first degree . . . It's clear that Sandra Lindsay and Deborah Johnson Dudley were killed as a result of being taken into that basement. It's clear that Gary Heidnik did it . . . It was premeditated. It was deliberate. It was intentional."

All anyone knew about Heidnik, he said, was what Heidnik had told them. "None of the experts can read a person's mind. None of them can tell when a person is lying. But I submit that you can tell. You all have common sense because you deal with people day in and day out."

Gallagher said Heidnik planned each of the abductions, choosing the women, "plying them with sex or food," choking them, handcuffing them, and chaining them in the basement.

He killed Lindsay and Dudley "in a cold, premeditated fashion," he said, and then disposed of Lindsay's body by dismembering it and cooking the parts that could lead to her identification—the head and the hands.

"Just because someone does bizarre acts, the law doesn't recognize them as insane . . . What he did was premeditated, deliberate murder."

He, too, had been pacing. Then he stopped and looked intently at the jurors. "Reject this defense," he said. "Reject the idea that this man is legally insane. Seek the truth, and I think you will find that this man, Gary M. Heidnik, is guilty beyond reasonable doubt of the specific intent to kill two young girls."

When he quit it was 12:49. His argument, by remarkable coincidence, had also taken precisely forty-five minutes.

Judge Abraham looked at the clock and announced that she was giving everyone the afternoon off. "I need to prepare my charge," she said, warning that it would be lengthy.

When Peruto finished his argument, he whispered to Heidnik as he slid into his chair, "How'd I do?" Heidnik simply grunted.

Then, after Gallagher's argument, when he was being led out of the courtroom back to a cell, Heidnik stopped when he was opposite Gallagher. Turning to Peruto, he said, "Your speech was better than his." The jurors were gone. They did not hear the remark.

Chapter 51

June 29, 1988

Overnight Room 653 was transformed from a courtroom into a classroom. Behind the judge's bench, where before there had been nothing, was a large green chalkboard and a three-foot-tall paper pad on an easel. Written on the top sheet of the pad, in large black letters, were the names of the captives. The chalkboard was blank.

"What is this?" Peruto wanted to know, referring to the equipment as "props."

"I always use these when I instruct a jury," said Judge Abraham. "You guys use charts and graphs to help you out, why shouldn't I?"

Before calling the jurors in, Abraham went through the usual morning ritual of discussing issues they didn't need to know about. The topic that morning was what she had included in her charge, that is, what suggestions she had culled from lists submitted by Gallagher and Peruto and what she had decided upon on her own. One thing she wanted to put before the jury was the issue of Josefina Rivera as a possible accomplice.

"I object to that," Gallagher said.

"Okay," Judge Abraham said amiably. "But I think it's an issue for the jury. It's not a question of law, but one of fact for the jury to decide."

To help make the jurors' job easier, Abraham added,

she had removed the misdemeanor charges from the list. "They'll merge with the felonies anyway," she pointed out.

It was almost ten-thirty. "Anyone who wants to leave the courtroom has to go now," the court crier announced. "No one will be allowed in or out during the judge's charge to the jury."

Abraham estimated it would take two hours. She was off by only half an hour.

Judge Abraham was in her glory; a captive audience and a chance to exercise her inherent pedantic tendencies. "Sometimes I may have to spell words to you that you've never heard before," she began condescendingly.

Walking over to the chalkboard, she scratched, PRESUMPTION OF INNOCENCE.

"The fact of Mr. Heidnik's arrest, the fact that charges have been filed against him, the fact that he is on trial, doesn't mean he's guilty. He is presumed innocent."

Her hand moved again. BRD, she wrote. "That means Beyond Reasonable Doubt—beyond the doubt that any reasonable person would consider. You must find Mr. Heidnik not guilty when the Commonwealth doesn't prove his guilt . . . you can't hold it against him because he did not testify . . . you have to assess the credibility of everyone in this case," she said, writing the word CREDIBILITY on the chalkboard. "That means believable."

Under *credibility* she wrote DEMEANOR.

"That means how they behave. It is part of the test of credibility."

She scratched, MOTIVE.

"Motive is a reason for testifying one way or the other," she said, adding an equal sign and the word *bias* beside *motive.*

* * *

At 11:25, an hour into the charge, she took a short recess. She still had not gotten to the crux of the matter. After the break, though, she plunged in.

"You have several options for verdicts," she said. "One is 'guilty.' Another is 'not guilty.' Another is 'not guilty by reason of insanity.' There is 'guilty but mentally ill.' Finally there is 'diminished capacity,' which is not really a verdict but an evidentiary issue, and it applies only to first-degree murder.

"A verdict of 'not guilty' means the state has failed to prove its case . . . To render a verdict of 'not guilty by reason of insanity' you must first conclude that he committed the crimes, but was *legally* insane . . . A verdict of 'guilty but mentally ill' means he is guilty beyond a reasonable doubt and he's not insane but mentally ill."

She explained that *insane* was a legal term, not a medical one. "Doctors use the term 'mental illness.' "

To be found legally insane, she said, Heidnik would have to meet the conditions set down in the M'Naghten Rule. "If at the time of the crime he is, as a result of mental disease, unable to know the nature and quality of his acts or unable to distinguish right from wrong, he meets the legal test. Otherwise, he is not legally insane."

A mental illness alone, she cautioned, cannot qualify someone as legally insane. And, she added, legal insanity must be proved by the defense by a preponderance of the evidence.

"Did Mr. Heidnik suffer from a mental disease or mental defect? Did he know what he was doing? Was he capable of doing it? If he knew what he was doing would cause injury or death, he knew the quality of his act. Did he know it was wrong?" These were questions they would have to answer, she said.

"If you first find him guilty, and the Commonwealth has proved he was sane but mentally ill at the time, he can be found guilty but mentally ill."

How do you know if someone is mentally ill? "If he lacks substantial capacity either to appreciate the wrongfulness of his conduct or is incapable of doing anything about it."

Diminished capacity kicks in, she added, only in first-degree murder. "That's where the defendant admits he committed the crime of murder but says he is not guilty because he was unable to meditate and couldn't form a specific intent to kill." In effect it lowers murder of the first degree to murder of the third degree. "If he had a fully formed intent to kill and was not laboring under a mental defect, then it's first degree."

Following another five-minute recess, she meticulously outlined the degrees of murder.

First-degree murder is premeditated. "The killer had a specific intent to kill. He was able to formulate a plan and carry it out.

"Second degree murder also is known as felony murder. That is when death occurs in some special felonies, such as arson, burglary, or *kidnapping.*" Since Heidnik was charged with multiple counts of kidnapping, she stressed that word. "The Commonwealth doesn't have to prove beyond a reasonable doubt that there was a specific intent to kill in second-degree murder," she said.

"Third-degree murder is where there is no intent to kill, but there is an intent to inflict grievous bodily harm."

She glanced at the clock again. "Let's all stretch," she said, standing and throwing her arms wide.

She was nearing the end now. In the next twenty minutes she raced through the other charges: rape, kidnapping, involuntary deviate sexual intercourse, and aggravated assault.

"Take your time," she told the jurors, "don't rush." It was one o'clock. Eat your lunch and then you can start deliberations, she said, sending them out of the room.

Peruto and Gallagher were to come back after lunch, she said, so they could work through the huge pile of exhibits, to determine what would be sent to the jury room as evidence. The state alone had filed almost two hundred items.

During the lunch hour two inmates unhappy with their day in court and looking for a victim jumped Heidnik while the three were alone in a holding cell. They beat him to his knees and were kicking him when the deputies heard the commotion and broke it up. He was not seriously injured. It was the second time since he was arrested that he had been attacked. Earlier, another inmate had smacked him in the face, breaking his nose.

Chapter 52

June 30–July 1, 1988

Waiting is never easy. While the Pittsburghers were off in a back room—presumably arguing, discussing, and sifting through documents—reporters, members of the captives' families, and a handful of diehard spectators loitered in the dreary hallway outside Room 653. Just about everybody, including Chuck Peruto, expected a quick verdict. The consensus also was that a quick verdict would be very bad for Gary Heidnik. But there was nothing quick about this jury. At five-thirty Judge Abraham told them to quit for the day.

The next morning, Friday, Abraham took pity on the crowd and opened the courtroom. It was better than the hallway. At least the hangers-on would have chairs and air-conditioning. Just before noon the jurors sent a note asking Judge Abraham for additional instructions. That required a gathering of all the participants: Abraham, Gallagher, Peruto, and, of course, Heidnik.

They had four questions, Abraham said.

1. What are the various degrees of murder?
2. At what point did Heidnik begin receiving one hundred percent disability?
3. What is legal insanity?
4. What is mental illness?

They would have to decide number 2 on their own, because that was a matter of fact for the jury to remember, Judge Abraham decided. In order to answer the other questions, she summoned them back into the courtroom. Again the doors were locked while she went through an abbreviated version of the charge she delivered the day before. It took an hour.

After the jury was sent back to argue some more, Judge Abraham looked at Peruto and Gallagher and shrugged. "The diminished-capacity provision is mumbojumbo," she acknowledged, "and the guilty-but-mentally-ill statute is not well-written. But that's the law. I didn't write the constitution. What do you want me to do?"

Peruto, not to be outdone in the quote department, praised the Pittsburgh jurors for their diligence. "The people in Philadelphia didn't even think he deserved a trial," he quipped, "much less deliberations." Pressed for a prediction, he smiled. "Something less than first degree."

Surely, veteran court watchers felt, the verdict would be forthcoming quickly now. Peruto was so confident that things were rolling, he hung around Room 653 for the rest of the afternoon, chatting with reporters and members of the victims' families. Although the family members had been hostile to him initially, they had warmed during the trial. Now they were feeling him out about representing them in possible suits against the hospitals that turned Heidnik loose. Philadelphia is a very litigious community.

Friday morning came and went. As the hours went by, Peruto's spirits rose. Surely they couldn't be out this long, he thought, if they were going to come back with a hanging verdict.

Finally, shortly after three o'clock, after about sixteen hours of deliberations over two and a half days, the jurors sent word that they were ready.

"I think it's going to be second degree," a grinning Peruto whispered to a reporter as the participants assembled.

Before the jurors were called in, Judge Abraham issued a stern warning to the spectators. No clapping, shouting, cheering, or crying. "There will be no expression of pleasure or displeasure," she cautioned, "under threat of contempt and immediate jailing." Reporters, too, would have to wait until the proceeding was over to leave the room.

When the jurors filed in, they looked grim and tired. Although they passed directly in front of Heidnik and Peruto, not one of them glanced at the defense table. That was a bad sign.

After aligning themselves in the jury box, a petite, brown-haired woman with a heart-shaped face and intelligent, dark eyes, identified herself as the foreperson. She was Betty Ann Bennett, a registered nurse married to a suburban Pittsburgh cop for twenty-two years. One by one she went down the list of charges: guilty in the first degree of murdering Deborah Dudley . . . guilty in the first degree of murdering Sandra Lindsay . . . guilty, guilty, guilty. Eighteen guilties: guilty on two counts of first-degree murder, five counts of rape, six counts of kidnapping, four counts of aggravated assault, and one count of involuntary deviate sexual intercourse. There was one acquittal—an involuntary deviate sexual intercourse charge involving Josefina Rivera. They gave no explanation for that finding.

When Peruto asked that they be polled, they stood individually and repeated the findings. Bennett, Kimberly Higgins—a young, single woman—and Marcella Lenhart, a bright-eyed brunette with three small children, appeared about to break into tears. But one juror, August Manfredo, glanced malevolently at Heidnik every time he said "guilty."

Peruto took it worse than Heidnik. When the first verdict of guilty of murder in the first degree was read, he deflated. He put his head in his hand and stared at the floor. Heidnik, on the other hand, didn't blink. He just sat upright, staring straight ahead, rhythmically pumping his legs.

The jury had returned at three-thirty. At 3:53, with the verdict read and the jurors polled, Judge Abraham called a brief recess.

As reporters scrambled out the door and dashed for the telephones, a deputy walked up to Heidnik and asked him if he wanted a glass of water. "No," he said quietly, still staring at the wall. Then he stood and put his hands behind his back to be cuffed. Still showing no emotion, he was led out of the room. When he came back, he pointedly stared at the area of the courtroom where the captives' family members had sat throughout the trial. And as he folded into his chair, he glanced over his shoulder and stared again in the same direction. It was the first indication he knew they were there. His gaze was not friendly.

Under Pennsylvania law a jury that returns a guilty verdict for first-degree murder must also set the penalty. They have two choices: life in prison, or death in the electric chair. It is a second, separate verdict requiring another immediate deliberation session. But before they could begin, the lawyers would have a chance to talk to the jury again, to argue aggravating and mitigating circumstances—their reasons for why he should or should not be sentenced to death. This procedure is called the penalty phase. Judge Abraham decreed it would begin at nine the next morning.

As the jurors marched out of the room, they again ignored Heidnik and Peruto. Some courthouse veterans noted this and commented that it did not bode well; that they may already have made up their minds about the punishment.

In the hallway the reporters clustered around Gallagher. "The jury rejected his plea of insanity," said the beaming DDA. "They decided this man had the specific intent to kill, and he did it with malice."

Peruto was in a rare morose mood. The jury acted emotionally, not intellectually, he said. "There is absolutely no evidence of first-degree murder. There's no question in my mind that Gary Heidnik is severely insane."

Chapter 53

July 2, 1988

The Saturday morning *Inquirer,* in three-quarter-inch letters across the top of the front page, screamed: HEIDNIK
IS CONVICTED OF MURDER. And, in smaller type, *His
plea of insanity is rejected by jury.* That almost guaranteed a fair crowd at the penalty session, even though it
was held early on a Saturday morning in the middle of
one of the most popular holiday weekends of the year.

With the jury still out of the room, Gallagher jumped
up to make one of his most forceful objections of the trial.
He questioned Judge Abraham's decision that allowed
Peruto to make the last argument before the jury began
deliberations. "The position of the Commonwealth is that
the Commonwealth always goes last," he asserted.

"It doesn't hurt the Commonwealth if it goes first and
the defense goes last in this situation," Abraham said.
"I'm going to stick to that."

Reluctantly, Gallagher sat down.

"In the penalty phase," the judge said, turning to
Peruto, "the defendant has the right to testify and call
witnesses, including his wife. Does he want to testify?"

"No, your honor," said Peruto.

"Does he want to call any witnesses?"

"No," Peruto repeated.

Peruto said earlier he was considering calling Betty

Heidnik. Indeed, she was in the courtroom that morning for the first time during the trial—an attractive, olive-skinned woman demurely dressed, hiding behind a pair of large, dark sunglasses. She sat in the back, with Dr. Clancy McKenzie, and left before the jury came back with its final verdict. Peruto said he decided not to call her because he was afraid her testimony would hurt him more than help him.

With the formalities taken care of, the jury was called in. They looked more rested, but the strain of the last few days was still clearly visible. They looked pale and grim, as if dreading the task still facing them. One man walked as though he were treading through a mine field; that the slightest misstep would result in disaster.

Gallagher began his final argument at 9:31. "The law isn't simple, but it's clear," he said. "If you find by unanimous decision that there are aggravating circumstances and no mitigating circumstances, the decision must be death."

Dressed in a conservative gray suit and solid white shirt, Gallagher paced slowly in front of the jury box.

"You've already found there was specific intent to kill Sandra Lindsay," he said. "She was chained, cuffed and naked, hung by her wrist for eight to twenty-four hours. She was not only mentally retarded, but she had trouble swallowing. She suffered from starvation and malnutrition. There is evidence to indicate she was beaten while she was hanging there . . . Gary Heidnik gave the other girls ice cream while Sandra Lindsay was hanging there. He said she was faking—a word he knows too well.

"In the case of Deborah Dudley," he continued, "she was tortured. She was taken upstairs and shown the remains of Sandra Lindsay's body and told to behave or it would happen to her. She was repeatedly beaten, a tape was put around her head, and screwdrivers were driven in her ears." Then, he added, she was killed.

"Don't rely upon leniency for this man or mercy for this man," he urged them. "Rely upon the evidence."

His speech lasted seventeen minutes. It was Peruto's turn.

"Before you sentence someone to die, it is my belief that you should know the whole picture," he began. "I can't argue what I know. I can't argue what Dr. Apsche knows. I can only argue the evidence.

"Look at him," he said, swiveling and pointing at Heidnik, who appeared oblivious to the situation. "He's full of Thorazine. His behavior today is not what it was like between November and March. When he formed, *fully* formed, his specific intent to kill either one of them—"

Judge Abraham interrupted. "You can't argue that at this point. That's already disposed of."

Thrown off stride, Peruto lowered his head and pinched the bridge of his nose between his thumb and forefinger. He stood that way for four or five seconds, looking defeated. Lifting his head, he turned to the jury and said softly: "I just hope you do the just thing and do not rely on procedural rules." Slowly, he returned to his chair and sat down. He had taken only four minutes.

Judge Abraham spent twenty-three minutes going over the details of deliberations with the jurors before sending them out to consider the options.

Fifteen minutes after the jury left the room, a court official whispered that they had ordered lunch. It looked like another long day. Peruto, ever the optimist, predicted they would not reach a verdict by Sunday evening and the judge would dismiss them and impose the mandatory life sentences.

He was wrong. At 12:10, only one hour and fifty-five minutes after they began deliberations, they sent word that they had a verdict.

After Heidnik was brought back in and took his seat,

Peruto turned and flashed him a questioning look. Heidnik just shrugged.

Betty Ann Bennett, looking grimmer than ever, stood and announced the decisions: death for the murder of Sandra Lindsay; death for the murder of Deborah Dudley.

"I thank you for your service, not for your decision," Judge Abraham said quickly.

Heidnik, as on the previous day, showed no emotion. Peruto winced, folded his arms on the table and laid his head down. He stayed that way for almost a minute. Gallagher sagged in relief.

Spectators had been warned again about demonstrations, so there were no overt displays. However, one of Lindsay's sisters sobbed silently.

Peruto stood and asked Judge Abraham to issue an order to prison officials to make sure Heidnik was kept in isolation. "If he is put in the general population, the jury's wishes will be carried out immediately," he said.

"If your client is going to commit suicide, he's going to do it," she said. "Prison officials don't want that, but neither do they want prisoners killing other prisoners. I don't have the authority to order him held in isolation, but I will suggest they carefully watch him for suicide and carefully house him."

To set the wheels in motion, she immediately sentenced Heidnik to death for Lindsay's murder and set a date three months in the future for sentencing on Dudley's killing.

Outside, Denise Dudley told reporters she was satisfied with the verdict. "My sister can rest in peace," she said. "We got what we wanted."

Lindsay's mother, Jeanette Perkins, said she was glad it was over. "I'm happy for what happened," she said, "because he sentenced my daughter to death."

Chapter 54

July 1988

Gary Heidnik spends most of his time sitting in his cell, staring at the wall. Sometimes, officials said, he reads his Bible. Not much else for him to do. His former recreational activities are a thing of the past. No more video games. No more movies. No more cars. No more women.

Since he is under death sentence—and since he lives constantly under threat of harm from other inmates—authorities at the State Correctional Institution at Pittsburgh keep him isolated. Prisoner number F1398 is confined to a cubicle by himself in a cell block referred to as a restricted housing unit. There are another hundred or so men in the section. Some of them are, like Heidnik, murderers, awaiting execution. Some are informers, put there for their own protection. And some of them are just plain mean. Too mean and generally too unfit for the company of others. For one reason or another they all are segregated.

But even among such a group Heidnik gets extra attention. When he showers, he does it alone. If he exercises, he does it alone. He eats his meals in his cell. Alone.

Isolation is a distinct form of punishment. But his punishment is also his protection. On his way to the Pittsburgh prison, when guards stopped the bus to transfer other inmates, Heidnik was left alone momentarily with other prisoners on the bus. As soon as the guards' backs were turned, they jumped him, and were still beating him when the guards rushed back to break it up. Such an incident, in prison slang, is called "a tuning up." Although Heidnik was not severely injured, when the other inmates finished with him, he was well tuned.

On the other hand, no one put him in a hole in the ground. No one beat him with shovel handles. No one dug in his ears with screwdrivers. And no one plugged him in to see if he shined like a floodlight at Three Rivers Stadium, a few minutes' walk away. Not yet anyway. It is ironic that his is one of the rare cases where the ultimate punishment coincidentially fits his crime. If he is electrocuted, he will die the same way his second victim, Deborah Dudley, died.

It is ironic, too, that he was assigned to a prison in Pittsburgh. Just on the other side of the wall are the men and women who convicted him; the men and women Heidnik came all the way across the state to pick to hear his defense. He was sent initially to the state's main prison at Graterford, near Philadelphia, for two weeks of probing, testing, and processing. What, if anything, the prison people discovered has not been disclosed. Probably nothing that has not already been regurgitated. Heidnik is a master at hiding things.

There are 1,600 men in SCI-Pittsburgh, and in varying degrees they all miss their freedoms. At no time, probably, is this more evident than on Sunday afternoons in autumn and early winter, when they can hear the crowds cheering the Steelers. Undoubtedly this sets off strong reminders of lost liberty. A mournful sound. The urban man's call of the wild goose. They remember what it was like to cheer a team. To drink a beer. To have a high time with a lady.

Nobody ever said anything about Gary Heidnik being a football fan. There was testimony that he drank only rarely and then very temperately. But the women! Gary Heidnik always had at least one woman in the house.

On the other hand, maybe thoughts of freedom are fleeting for Gary Heidnik. He has been in one institution or another since he was fourteen. It began when he assumed the rigid discipline of military school. Then he went into the Army. His story is, he didn't want to leave. Then he didn't want to leave the hospitals. Perhaps now he's finding a home behind the walls. At least one psychiatrist who treated him during his chain of hospitalizations noted that Heidnik was becoming excessively institutionalized. Now he is institutionalized in spades.

This time, though, he's not in the military. Not in a hospital where he can check himself in or out. Where he can slip away AMA—Against Medical Advice. He's not even back in Farview, or one of the institutions where his girlfriend used to visit him and they'd get it on in the ladies room; in the elevator; in the bushes. He's in a real prison now. Not exactly hard time, but close enough.

Still one more irony is that, despite his imprisonment, his income continues: $1,212 every month from the VA, and another $708 in Social Security. It goes into a bank account watched over by the courts. He has no place to spend it.

A few reporters wrote him asking for interviews. He turned them down. While he was still at Graterford he had two visitors one day: Betty and his infant son J.J. Whether they will travel across the state to see him has yet to be seen.

Gary Heidnik's prospects of ever getting out of prison are zilch. The best he can hope for is to have his death sentences lifted or be transferred to a mental hospital. If he lives that long. Some don't think he will. Chuck Peruto for one.

After the closing arguments, but before the case went to the jury last June, a glum Peruto slumped behind the marble pedestal desk in his office and unburdened himself

of his melancholy thoughts. Gary Heidnik didn't stand a
snowball's chance in hell of getting any mercy, he figured. Even, *even,* if he was not sentenced to die, Heidnik
was at the end of his road, Peruto said.

"I'll make a prediction," he volunteered. "I predict
Gary Heidnik's going to kill himself. I predict he'll be
dead before your book hits the stands."

The question no one was able to answer—in fact,
which no one even addressed—was why Gary Heidnik
was on the street to begin with. Ten years previously,
Judge Mirarchi had sensed impending catastrophe and
sent Heidnik away for as long as he could. Other psychiatrists subsequently recommended that he not be released.
Certainly he had drawn the attention of law enforcement
officials and mental health authorities more than once.
Yet he was unconfined.

Part of the problem undoubtedly is a result of the
tension that exists between the courts and mental health
professionals. There was no disagreement during Heidnik's trial that psychiatry is an inexact science. But
viewed in the light of what occurred, that term becomes
meaningless. To say that the majority of the conclusions
about Heidnik were "inexact" is a tremendous under-
statement. To say they were based on science is even
more ludicrous. If those diverse opinions are among the
best the "science" can offer, there is only one conclusion:
judging the degree of someone's mental illness is guesswork.

The demands of the criminal justice system contribute
to the confusion. The law wants absolutes. Psychiatry
cannot produce them. Unhappily, a solution is not on the
horizon. Twenty-six states still use M'Naghten as the formal test for legal insanity. M'Naghten was promulgated
145 years ago. Since then, apparently, there have not
been sufficient advancements in psychiatry to devise a
more reliable indicator of a person's mental state. We

simply don't know what makes a man like Gary Heidnik tick. Even more frightening is the comprehension that no one—not the police, not the courts, not the mental health people—knows how many other Gary Heidniks are out there.

Epilogue

In the aftermath:

• Josefina Rivera, Lisa Thomas, Jacquelyn Askins, and Agnes Adams melted back into their pre-Heidnik existences. All the captives, and Heidnik's wife Betty, as well, are protected from reporters by a screen of attorneys they have hired to get part of the money in the Merrill Lynch account.

• *Philadelphia Daily News* reporter Maria Gallagher telephoned Michael Heidnik, Gary's father. She asked him if he wanted to know what the verdict was. "I'm not interested," he said. "I don't care. It don't bother me a bit. All I want is for you people to leave me alone. I don't care what happens."

• Chuck Peruto went straight from Heidnik's trial to another homicide case. He looked back on the trial with some bitterness, claiming the jury was too overwhelmed by the viciousness of Heidnik's acts to objectively view the evidence of his insanity. He filed notice of appeal, citing alleged errors by Judge Lynne Abraham in, among other things, allowing DDA Gallagher to introduce material through Peruto's witnesses, Jack Apsche and Kenneth Kool, that the defense attorney was prohibited from presenting. Despite his efforts, he was pessimistic about the chances for a second trial. "Heidnik was lucky to get one trial," he commented cynically, "there's no way he's going to get another."

• Charles Gallagher continued to lambast Heidnik. "Is Gary Heidnik crazy?" he echoed in response to a question. "Crazy like a fox! He has a personality disorder. He has a medical problem. But he's not legally insane. He definitely is not suffering from any major mental illness." To what did he attribute his victory? "I thought I destroyed any evidence the defense presented." On several talk shows afterwards, Gallagher made an issue of saying he was the only one who knew the "real" Heidnik, but he was so restricted by the system that he could not present the "whole story." He and police lieutenant James Hansen were considering writing a book about the case.

• Tony Brown, Heidnik's friend and former driver, was pronounced a free man. Two weeks after Heidnik's conviction, at Gallagher's request, Judge Charles L. Durham dismissed all charges against him.

• The federal bankruptcy judge is not expected to make any decision on the complicated case until well into 1989. In addition to the victims, the Peace Corps is seeking some of the funds, and the IRS is looking to see if the bulk of the money should not go to the government for taxes. These proceedings may delve into the question of the legitimacy of the church. Was Gary Heidnik religiously motivated? Was it a tax scam?—questions that were not addressed during the criminal trial.

• Judge Lynne Abraham declined to be interviewed about the Heidnik case, citing the danger it might present to the appeals process. Gallagher on the judge: "Her rulings were right down the middle. She was a good judge in that I wanted to do some things for the Commonwealth, but she wouldn't let me." Peruto: "If I had any other judge, I might have won this case."

• Dr. Jack Apsche began work on another case for Peruto and was making plans to enroll in law school.

• Dr. Clancy McKenzie was trying to find a lawyer to represent him in a slander action against Peruto for calling him a "flake."

• An official appraiser hired by the city examined Heidnik's house at 3520 North Marshall Street and evaluated the three-bedroom, one-bath dwelling at $3,000, which was $12,900 less than he paid for it in 1983 and $11,000 less than he still owes on it. Repairs—including a new roof, replacement of broken windows, and filling in holes in the basement floor—would cost an estimated $15,000. In a separate note, the appraiser wryly added: the estimated value "does not account for possible market resistance due to any stigmatization that may be caused by the notoriety of alleged acts committed on the premises by the current owner."

Among the stacks of documents and pieces of information that did not get an airing at the trial, one of the most revealing was a fifteen-page typewritten manuscript composed by Heidnik under the appropriate pseudonym "Gary Bishop." Entitled "Fortieth Street Soaps or Life in the Slow Lane," it appears to be the beginning of a book. It has a title page, a dedication (to Shirley Carter), a prologue, and twelve pages called "Chapter One." It is about the underground culture that thrives in the neighborhood of Fortieth and Market Streets, around the Elwyn Institute. It talks about the disadvantaged—the mentally and physically handicapped—who rely on each other for support, companionship, and love.

In the story, the author-protagonist, obviously Heidnik, is reemerging into the world after more than four years in state hospitals for the criminally insane. It tells how he goes to stay with a friend he identifies as John, probably his old friend, John Francis Cassidy. In the story the author spends some time with an old girl-friend (Carter?). He shops for a van. He goes to see his old friends at McDonald's. He becomes attached to his host's strange cat. It is a rambling story, going nowhere really. But it is an upbeat tale, not a depressing one. While it no doubt accurately reflects what was happening in Heidnik's life at the time, it does not go into the past or give any indication what was going to happen in the future.

Another revealing tidbit was a brief interview with Albert Leavitt, a psychologist for the Common Pleas Court. Leavitt's colleagues twice examined Heidnik, giving him a full battery of tests.

"Do you think Heidnik is crazy?" I asked.

Leavitt paused for a moment. "Let me put it this way," he said. "If there were an Olympics for craziness, Heidnik would be a gold-medal winner."

He's not just manipulating the system?

"He's not manipulating anything. He's absolutely stone crazy."

In Leavitt's opinion, Heidnik is on the same level as Charles Manson and Jim Jones, the charismatic leader who set up an ill-fated colony in Jonestown, British Guiana. Heidnik should be put under a microscope, Leavitt said, because he is the rare perfect example of an insane person as defined by M'Naghten.

Twenty-one times Gary Heidnik entered mental health facilities. Twenty-one times he was discharged. Even when he said he wasn't ready to go. Even when he begged to stay.

The truth is, Gary Heidnik should never have been free. If some of the people he came into contact with—

just the people he met during the four-month period in which he was holding the captives—had been a little more perceptive, a little less cautious, a tad less cynical, a smidgen less bureaucratic, Sandra Lindsay and Deborah Dudley might be alive.

If Sergeant Armstrong had carried his investigation into Sandra Lindsay's disappearance just one step further . . . if Officer Aponte had shown a little more curiosity about what Heidnik was cooking for dinner . . . if Dr. Hole had been a little more searching in his examination and a little less anxious to dash off a prescription . . . if Judge Levin, during the hearing in family court, had followed his instincts a little more closely . . . the story may have had a different ending.

A Cellar Chronology

November 26, 1986 — Gary Heidnik offers Josefina Rivera twenty dollars for sex, takes her home and makes her his first captive.

November 29, 1986 — Sandra Lindsay, an old friend of Heidnik's, is taken captive and joins Rivera in the basement.

December 22, 1986 — Heidnik picks up teenager Lisa Thomas, woos her with a cheeseburger and clothing from Sears, and locks her in the cellar.

January 1, 1987 — Deborah Dudley becomes number four.

January 18, 1987 — Eighteen-year-old Jacquelyn Askins becomes the youngest member of the horror harem.

February 7, 1987 — Sandra Lindsay dies. Heidnik dismembers her body; tries to destroy parts of it by cooking.

March 18, 1987 —Deborah Dudley is electrocuted. Heidnik stores her body in his basement freezer, alongside the ice cream.

March 22, 1987 —Heidnik disposes of Dudley's body by dumping it in a New Jersey park.

March 23, 1987 —Heidnik and Josefina Rivera pick up Agnes Adams and add her to the captives group.

March 24-25, 1987 —Rivera escapes and goes to police. Heidnik arrested.

June 20, 1988 —Heidnik goes on trial for killing Lindsay and Dudley, plus multiple charges of kidnapping, rape, aggravated assault, involuntary deviate sexual intercourse, and others.